"Stress-Free Performance Appraisals turns the writing of such appraisals from a tedious paperwork chore to a powerful management and motivational tool—a valuable new way of thinking about an old task."

—Robert Bly, author, *101 Ways to Make Every Second Count* (Career Press)

"A breath of fresh air around an old subject. Full of exceedingly helpful tips, insights, guidelines, and tools. A keeper for managers and employees alike—and for every manager who wants to keep talent on the team. We finally have the what, why, how, and wherefore of performance appraisal...all in one place."

—Beverly Kaye, Founder/CEO Career Systems International, co-author: *Love 'Em or Lose 'Em: Getting Good People to Stay*

"It's rare to find a book on performance appraisals that is so well-researched, entertainingly written, and packed full of real-life examples. This user-friendly guide is written in an easy-to-understand, practical way. It's not only a highly valuable tool for the HR professional and the operating manager, but one that will be particularly useful for the employee—the too-often-neglected beneficiary of a good performance appraisal procedure."

—Dick Grote, President, Grote Consulting Corporation and author of *The Complete Guide to Performance Appraisal* and *The Performance Appraisal Question and Answer Book*

"A much needed, easily readable book about an extremely valuable management tool. This book tells why and how good performance evaluations help a business retain its best employees. Using anecdotes and well documented studies, it examines the fears and misconceptions preventing many employers from using evaluations to maintain an effective workforce. This book should be required reading for all employers and their supervisors."

—Henry P. Baer, former Chair of the Labor & Employment Law Practice, Skadden, Arps, Slate, Meagher & Flom LLP, an international law firm

Stress-free
Performance
Appraisals

Turn Your Most Painful
Management Duty Into a
Powerful Motivational Tool

Sharon Armstrong
Madelyn Appelbaum

CAREER
PRESS

Franklin Lakes, N.J.

STRESS-FREE PERFORMANCE APPRAISALS
EDITED BY KATE HENCHES
TYPESET BY EILEEN DOW MUNSON
Cover design by DesignConcept
Printed in the U.S.A. by Book-mart Press

To order this title, please call toll-free 1-800-CAREER-1 (NJ and Canada: 201-848-0310) to order using VISA or MasterCard, or for further information on books from Career Press.

B CAREER
P PRESS

The Career Press, Inc., 3 Tice Road, PO Box 687,
Franklin Lakes, NJ 07417
www.careerpress.com

Library of Congress Cataloging-in-Publication Data

Armstrong, Sharon, 1951-
  Stress-free performance appraisals : turn your most painful management duty into a powerful motivational tool / by Sharon Armstrong and Madelyn Appelbaum.
    p. cm.
  Includes index.
  ISBN 1-56414-686-3 (paper)
    1. Employees—Rating of. I. Appelbaum, Madelyn. II. Title.

HF5549.5.R3A76 2003
658.3'125—dc21

2003053265

Acknowledgments

To the many who shared their stories, from the boardroom to the water cooler, and from both sides of the desk, we are very grateful. Along with the angst about performance appraisals, there was an eager willingness to do them right. Just as effective appraisals, our colleagues contributed measurably to the dialogue, clarified the landscape, and inspired a framework that most values each organization's most essential assets—the ones that go home every night.

Our thanks to Michael Strand, Diane Gold, and Brent Charbonneau for so willingly lending their considerable skills; Erin Barclay for dogged, talented reporting; Priscilla Vazquez, Gaye Newton, Patricia Bicknell, and Kristi Patrice Carter for key research support; and especially Irene Cardon, the continuing bright light in a not always shining development process. Literary agent, Marilyn Allen, understood the need, despite a Mt. Everest of personnel tomes, to cut through to the basics of what makes a performance appraisal fly.

Our families listened patiently. To Richard, for spirited editing, Margaret, Wendy, and Jill, we give our loving thanks.

S.A. & M.A

Washington, D.C.

May 1, 2003

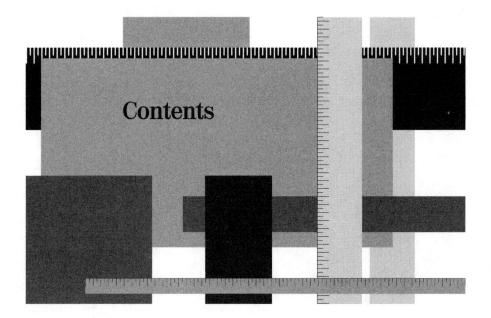

Contents

It's Not Supposed to Be This Way...

Performance appraisals can be one of the most anxiety-provoking aspects of work—for both supervisors and employees. Appraisals are meant to be clear, rewarding, interactive, and fair. They take real time, real dialogue, and a real focus on the future—not just the previous months. And they need to work successfully for all employees—not just the terrific ones!

Yet often that's not how it works. Supervisors tell of too much focus on tedious written forms and too little training, of "just getting through it," of getting hit with lawsuits or complaints when there's even a hint about "improvement opportunities," and of the difficulties of measuring intangibles. Employees often just plain dread appraisals, citing feelings of trepidation from a "once a year necessary evil," hostility over having "one error dragged through 10 categories," and frustration with "perfunctory" appraisals that neither acknowledge nor foster growth. As one employee put it, "The perception of the individual or relationship often dictates how critical or complementary a supervisor will be." Without clear baselines, measurable parameters, and organization-wide accountability, performance appraisals are, by nature, subjective judgments that are arbitrary and all over the map.

With a multitude of approaches, "appraising" appears to be an inevitable fact of life since the dawn of recorded history and predictably well before. Many workplace strategies now heralded as "new" began in the mid-1800s.[1] Performance evaluation as a distinct management procedure came decades later, and then mainly as pay-for-performance. In the beginning, the procedure was rather simple. Workers were paid for measurable output. "Piece rate" pay systems compensated workers in proportion to their productivity.[2] An entire era of incentive schemes emerged, and while standards of output could be defended on a more systematic basis, and pay could be more clearly linked to an individual's performance, a key question remained: Why did employees persist in certain traditional practices and not respond to the cash nexus?[3]

As behavioral science came into prominence in the mid-1950s, a more modern model of performance appraisals began to take shape and, with attention to morale and self-esteem, appraisals grew in promise as tools of motivation and development. To this day, there is controversy over if and how appraisals should be tied to financial reward. Pay raises or cuts do not necessarily improve or even sustain job effectiveness. And clearly employees with roughly equal capabilities can receive the same pay yet perform at very different levels.

Strong advocates view appraisals as potentially "...the most crucial aspect of organizational life."[4] Others question the value of appraisals, suggesting the process is so inherently flawed it may be impossible to perfect.[5] In between are clear endorsements for using performance appraisals, but wide-ranging disagreement on how.

What is also clear is that performance appraisals are all over the workplace. They can be conducted fairly, comprehensively, confidentially, and productively. This book is loaded with such examples. But they can also occur on the phone, on the run, or during a chance meeting on the elevator. They can be open-ended, or a checklist of items that don't even relate to on-the-job functions. They can also be late, often not conducted until well into the next work year. Performance indicators may not be uniform throughout an organization, specific job levels, or even in the same department.

Why is such a shabby face so often put on one of the most vital and continuing workplace responsibilities? In the mid-90s, a survey by the Council of Communication Management confirmed what almost every employee already knows—that recognition for a job well done is *the* top motivator of employee performance.[6] Via formal evaluations and through regular informal routes, performance appraisals yield excellent opportunities to motivate. Yet the process is frequently counterproductive, or viewed merely as perfunctory, almost as an aside. Maybe this is because we just don't know how to do performance appraisals well. Rather than an ongoing process, or number of mini-meetings, performance appraisals have become *an annual event*, one that strikes at the vulnerable cores of supervisors and employees alike.

It's not supposed to be this way. Rather than a painful yearly event, performance appraisals can be viewed as a discussion, a culmination of small meetings held throughout the evaluation period. The appraisals can be shaped objectively, according to clear standards about the quality of employee performance. Appraisals can clarify present expectations, track future ones and underscore the importance of two-way feedback. They can work to engage employees in their own career development. And happily, the elements involved (goal-setting, effective observation, practical documentation, and ongoing communications) can all be learned. In this book you'll find Supervisors' and Employees' Self-Assessments and other tools. You'll find sound guidelines and helpful insights for use on both sides of the desk. There are critical do's and don'ts, tips for "owning" the appraisal, and ways to leverage it.

In one form or other, performance reviews will continue to be a fact of our work life. This book is designed to cut through all the anxiety and make the process—or series of discussions—more pleasant and productive. It's also designed to bring performance appraisals into the 21st century, including such areas as job-sharing, telecommuting, RIFs, shared supervision, team evaluations, nerve-wracking economic forecasts, legal concerns, and accommodating particular employee challenges.

The chapters tap into the actual feelings of employees and their bosses as they seek out balance and structure, travel the steps to successful appraisals, craft discussions that won't bite, develop measurable goals, link to organizational vision, and keep to the right side of the law. You'll find good examples and painful ones, real-life performance appraisal problems and support in handling them. There are many hallmarks of painless reviews, and a route to tossing appraisals out completely.

The aim here is to remove the dread from performance evaluations. Conducting/receiving them need no longer be one of the worst days of your work year.

The Roots of Anxiety

1

No matter how "scientific," no matter even how many insights it produces, an appraisal that focuses on "potential," on "personality," on "promise"—on anything that is not proven and provable performance—is an abuse.

—Peter Drucker, often called the "most important managment thinker of our time."

Enter the fast heartbeat. Despite the fact that so many of us have experienced performance appraisals for years—often on both sides of the desk—even asking about them usually brings grimaces. Whether appraisals are glowing or, more frequently, just non-events, both supervisors and their staffs alike tend to frame them negatively, conjuring up images of "being called to the principal's office," "getting hit with a bad surprise," and "engaging in a sham." A supervisor may be worried about being "perceived as the enemy" because she gave a candid review. A mid-level employee said he wanted "constructive criticism" but was anxious because he didn't know what it would be. One employee simply said, "I hate being judged, and that's all appraisals really are."

U.S. Secretary of State, General Colin Powell, is clear about what he appraises: "Intelligence and judgment and, most critically, a capacity to anticipate, to see around corners; also, loyalty, integrity, a high energy drive, a balanced ego, and the drive to get things done."[1]

It's usually not that clear.

Definitions of modern-day performance appraisals generally run along these lines: As an important element of performance management, appraisals are yearly or semi-annual formal interactions between employees and their direct supervisors during which employees' strengths and weaknesses are cited and goals are assessed and set. As indicated in Chapter 3, performance appraisals take multiple routes.

Ideally, the appraisal is a two-way discussion and strengths and weaknesses are considered within the context of organizational goals. There are goals set jointly at the start of that year's performance cycle that form the basis of discussion. The appraisal is constructive, distinct from talk about compensation and a "no surprise" evaluation that reflects a series of discussions or mini-reviews conducted throughout the year. And, for good reason, Peter Drucker, in his landmark book, *The Practice of Management*, postpones discussion of financial rewards until nearly the end, explaining that "financial rewards are not major sources of positive motivation in the modern industrial society, even though discontent with them inhibits performance. The best economic rewards are not substitutes for responsibility or for the proper organization of the job."[2] It appears best to postpone discussion about pay until after the review. Veering off to a discussion about pay upfront can divert attention from the work performance itself.

The path to the ideal can be rocky. For a process that's so well established in the corporate landscape, the performance appraisal is astonishingly unpopular. Employees dread it as an annual calling to account...managers see it as a bureaucratic chore. According to the (United Kingdom's) Institute of Personnel and Development, one in eight managers would actually prefer to visit the dentist than carry out a performance appraisal.[3]

■ ■ ■ ■ ■ ■ ■ ■ ■ ■ ■ ■

Supervisors' Perspectives

- ◨ Delivering bad news is painful.
- ◨ There's never time to prepare.
- ◨ It's hard to measure intangibles.
- ◨ There's no accountability, so why bother.

▣ No training or guidance is given.

▣ There's forced ranking—bell curve is more important than employees.

▣ Forms are as heavy as the St. James version of the Bible.

▣ Employees only want to get to money part.

▣ It's hard to distinguish between criticism and professional development.

▣ Employees may come up with surprises.

▣ It's tough to be objective with well-liked employees.

Employees' Perspectives

▣ It's a meaningless exercise.

▣ Emphasis is on form, not process.

▣ Surprises are scary.

▣ They're always late, even when raises are attached.

▣ Supervisors just want to get through them.

▣ There's always one negative area, then little about anything else.

▣ It's never a two-way discussion.

▣ Basis for measurement is fuzzy.

▣ A "meets expectations" rating is like getting a "C"...no matter what my supervisor says.

▣ My boss has no real understanding of what I do every day.

■ ■ ■ ■ ■ ■

Natural and Cultural Drivers

Why are appraisals so troublesome, especially when performance evaluations are as old as life itself? Almost any program on the Discovery Channel provides compelling evidence that all life is wired to perform them. Every species has its most accomplished leaders, hunters, and more desirable mates. In nature, performance appraisals are a fascinating and instinctive truth of daily life.

Human performance appraisals, of course, are not as beautifully programmed. But culturally driven, appraisals appear to be a fact of human history. Perhaps the earliest record is derived from the Code of Hammurabi (circa 18th century B.C.), which gave the green light to pay-for-performance to some of Babylonia's traveling merchants. Their income went up just as soon as they brought in double the principals' investment for their services. Shortfalls were made up from their own funds.[4] Appraisals have also been pivotal in shaping history. Spanish colonizers appraised Indian societies by their cooperation, cultural-linguistic affiliation, and locality. "Tribes" were imagined, then created for administrative purposes. Categories that were later adopted by English colonizers, anthropologists, and government officials, then cemented by the reservation system, are a basis for present-day tribal identities.[5] Inspired by a powerful dramatist, ideal Samurai virtues, such as honor and loyalty, have been widely revered in Japanese society since at least the late 17th century. The disgrace of dishonor remains powerful to this day.[6] Performance appraisals are also potent outside of the cubicle. Hindu marriages, for example, are considered a union of two families, not merely two people, and bloodlines and reputations definitely matter.[7] Performance appraisals occur—family-style. The same is true of many other cultures.

Performance appraisals do not begin or end in the workplace. Where our children attend day care, the medical care we choose, where we work and shop are all grounded in an evaluation process. But unlike a work situation, we usually feel more in control—we are doing the judging, not having, as one mid-level attorney put it, "an annual check-up where the doctor doesn't have the blood work to measure how I'm really doing."

Emotional Framework

On-the-job performance appraisals will inevitably be underscored by human dynamics. The approach may be tested, piloted, considered, and replaced by another approach. But it will inescapably be a mix of subjective judgments/reactions, emotions, flashbacks to experiences that reinforce or dispel, and all the expectations and anxieties that frame the appraisal session itself. This book is a roadmap to first acknowledge, then cut through all that. Understanding what's causing all the fast heartbeats is a useful first step.

For starters, performance appraisals tap into a hefty smorgasbord of emotions. But please ditch any notion that, on either side of the desk, emotions get sanitized simply because they surface in the workplace. While this book supports routes to getting and staying on the right track to effective performance appraisals, it does so in the context of human frailties and vulnerabilities. Consider the "no surprise" performance appraisal that workers aspire to have and supervisors desire to give. Human beings have a distinct dislike for uncertainty. Maslow's groundbreaking needs theory developed in 1943 lists safety as just the second rung of a five-stage hierarchy of needs. This need covers "not just physical safety but questions about job security and organizational practices," [8] striking at the heart of our comfort zones.

■ ■ ■ ■ ■ ■ ■ ■ ■ ■ ■ ■ ■

What We Fear?[15]

Failure

A steadfast staple on fear lists, the fear of failing, is perhaps grounded in the notion that everything we do must be successful, and that there's no truth to thinking that there's no such thing as a genuine failure if we grow from it.

Success

Ranked almost as high as the fear of failure, success is often something we have no guidelines for—we may prepare for failure, but not for success. Yet success frequently means more responsibility, more attention, more stress, continued pressure to perform as well or even better, diversion from other priorities, and sometimes increased liability.

Judgment

Just about everyone grows up seeking approval from parents, teachers, and peers—and there's no reason to think that desiring positive feedback from others changes in adulthood. That's why recognition from others consistently shows up as the prime key to motivation. Yet shaping our lives by external perspectives leaves little room to discover and go after those dreams and goals that are truly ours. Judging others, and allowing them to judge us, drains emotion, aspiration, time, and energy.

Emotional Pain

Life is loaded with lessons that teach and spur growth—unless we get stuck in the hurt and negativity that block personal and professional gratification. Knowing the difference between a "let down" and a continuing roadblock is essential.

Embarrassment

Even more embarrassing than private screw-ups, public mistakes are...well, public. But everyone who deals with people sometimes makes them. Handling them gracefully, rectifying the damage, and moving on is the way to go. Tapping into just about all of these fears, the only alternative to fear of embarrassment is to stay stuck in the mistake.

Sharing Our True Feelings

Young children are clear about their feelings. But as adults, we must sometimes learn, through practice, how to be open and honest. For starters, it's important to be clear to ourselves how we feel about a particular issue. If we don't know, it's important to find out. Being honest, especially in a situation perceived as threatening, can be tough. Open and honest may not be easy, but it offers a clear track for moving ahead rather than continually navigating a series of perilous curves. Employers can set the standard by shaping a work site that expects honesty and creates a safe harbor for practicing it.

The Unknown

Key to appraisal anxiety is the fear of being surprised, especially when evaluations are a yearly event rather than a series of mini-reviews. Effectively preparing for them as suggested in Chapter 2, being attentive to work output all year long, and asking periodically for feedback, even if it's not offered, will go a long way toward dousing the "mights" and "what ifs" that often shadow the anticipation of performance appraisals.

Intimacy

Being open and honest means being yourself, revealing who you are and what you feel with another human being or, in work situations, with multiple other beings. How open and honest these multiple others will be with you is a product of the work climate, the individuals drawn to it, and your own behavior. While there are, of course, clear boundaries on the level of openness and sharing at work, showing up should not require an emotional costume—it's reasonable to expect to be yourself, keeping your standards, values, and comfort levels intact.

Being Rejected/Alone/Abandoned

Being yourself should be a positive aspect of work. Test it before predetermining that your talents, ideas, and solutions won't be accepted, or that you'll be perceived as "dumb" or shown the door. Ease into becoming more participatory, pilot your ideas with a trusted colleague and then your boss, team up on projects and offer to take on more responsibility. Before long you'll be a real player—but probably too busy to notice.

■ ■ ■ ■ ■ ■

This book is also written with the trust that "gut feelings" are a valid compass in approaching appraisals. In his engaging book, *The Emotional Brain*, New York University science professor Joseph LeDoux traces many emotions as "products of evolutionary wisdom, which probably has more intelligence than all human minds together." He cites evolutionary psychologists who believe that our species' past goes a long way toward explaining our present individual emotional state.[9] LeDoux also cites the work of Isaac Marks in highlighting the "striking extent" to which protective strategies apply across the various vertebrates. When danger is perceived, just a few strategies are called into play: withdrawal, immobility, defensive, aggressive, and submission.[10] Why does this read like a Dilbert cartoon?

Dilbert reprinted by permission of United Feature Syndicate, Inc.

By nature and nurture, we are wired to react as we do. Understandable or not, we still have to deal with both our behavior and its consequences. Ask supervisors and their staffs about handling appraisals—and modes of avoidance rise high on the list. But avoidance as a symbolic foxhole usually can't last for an entire year. The appraisal inevitably occurs, even if it's six months late.

It doesn't help that the disconnect between what tends to count most to employees and what supervisors think counts most to employees seems to be rather dramatic. Despite changing conditions, site studies first conducted by the Labor Relations Institute of New York in 1946, and then repeated in 1981 and 1994, reinforced that, as top motivators, white-collar nonsupervisory employees most valued "full appreciation for work done," followed closely by "feeling in" on things. In 1946, these values ranked first and second respectively; then eased into second and third place respectively in 1981 and 1994 when "interesting work" topped the list. In all three studies, "good wages" ranked only fifth of 10 factors. When immediate supervisors were asked what motivated their employees, they ranked good wages first, job security second, and promotion/growth opportunities third,[11] a ranking that stayed constant in all three studies.

■ ■ ■ ■ ■ ■ ■ ■ ■ ■ ■ ■ ■

What People Want From Their Work[16]

Employee Ranking		Supervisor Ranking
1	Full appreciation of work done	8
2	Feeling of being in on things	10
3	Sympathetic help on personal problems	9
4	Job security	2
5	Good wages	1
6	Interesting work	5
7	Promotion and growth in the organization	3
8	Personal loyalty to employees	6
9	Good working conditions	4
10	Tactful disciplining	7

■ ■ ■ ■ ■ ■ ■

Failure to Motivate

With such wide variance, it is not surprising that employees are often less certain about where they stand after the appraisal than before it, tend to evaluate supervisors less favorably afterwards, and often report that few constructive actions or significant improvements resulted. In 2001, an international survey of 8,000 employees and managers revealed that one-third of employees reported that their managers provided little or no assistance in improving their performance—and that they had never even had a formal discussion with their managers regarding overall performance.[12] And there's no overstating that it is not just employees but also their bosses who disparage organizational evaluation practices. Second only to firing an employee, managers cite performance appraisals as the task they dislike the most.[13] As a long-time appraisal navigator put it: "As an employee, I'd rather be in the dentist's chair." As a supervisor, I think, "Isn't there something more important to do today...like budget planning?" Despite careful preparation, I'm always afraid I'll screw the appraisal up."

When we wondered why Hallmark hadn't yet tapped into such widespread angst, ad whiz Ed Avant shot back with this:

You're wondering what your rating is
I haven't told you all year long
Now it's time to tell you
All the things that you've done wrong!

Except that it's a serious personal and organizational matter. Every performance appraisal that fails to motivate, or worse, is a lost opportunity for both the employee and the employer. Aristotle was perhaps the first to observe that: "We are what we repeatedly do." Each employee evaluation that neglects to recognize actual employee performance serves to perpetuate weaker qualities and omit reinforcing the positive. Morale, employee esteem, and organizational interests get doused in the process. One banking employee said that her once-a-year perfunctory appraisal only reinforced that she was a "9-to-5 fixture and not a real human being." That talented employee has since advanced quickly in a wiser financial institution.

Early career issues are a sensitive matter, too. While young people are often disappointed by the nature of their first work assignments at the bottom of an organization, they still believe they are doing an exemplary job. Therefore, many are surprised and disappointed by the results of their initial performance appraisals. With their managers focused primarily on those areas most in need of correction, these young workers are caught up in examples and illustrations of poor performance, yielding appraisals somewhat more negative than originally envisioned.[14] Thus a sour taste from the start.

The following pages are designed to help change this sour taste, to help you widen the lens, step back from particular incidents and concerns, and to focus on the broader, brighter picture—an approach more gratifying than appraisal anxiety.

■ ■ ■ ■ ■ ■ ■ ■ ■ ■ ■ ■

Why Do Performance Appraisals?

▣ Two-way performance feedback.

▣ Recognition for individual performance.

▣ Motivational tool when used effectively.

▣ Goal-setting for next review period in context of organizational/departmental needs.

▣ Opportunity to reinforce and document personnel decisions.

▣ Opportunity to demonstrate organizational fairness to all employees.

▣ Opportunity to support individual needs.

▣ Opportunity to reinforce continuing open communication/ strengthen rapport.

▣ Opportunity to spur independent thinking plus avenues of teamwork.

▣ Opportunity to encourage employees to take responsibility for their work.

▣ Opportunity to contribute to organizational effectiveness.

▣ Opportunity to discover untapped potential...on both sides of the desk.

■ ■ ■ ■ ■ ■ ■

These self-assessments are designed to pinpoint areas of particular interest or concern. Certain responses may serve as a wake-up call, providing insight that can help you focus on these areas in the following chapters that will be most useful to you.

Self-Assessment for Supervisors

How do you rate yourself on the following? (1 = very often; 5 = not at all)

Provide timely feedback on a regular basis. _____

Carefully plan and prepare for the performance appraisal discussion. _____

Hold the performance discussion when it's expected. _____

Pull specific examples to support ratings. _____

Ensure that all appraisal discussions are private and confidential. _____

Set aside an appropriate amount of time to have a meaningful exchange. _____

Let my employees know how much I value their work. _____

Have a clear understanding of my organization's mission/goals. _____

Review the completed form for fairness prior to the meeting. _____

Encourage two-way communication. _____

Take into account my employees' needs and goals as we plan the future. _____

Offer viable suggestions for improvement and development.

Separate the discussion of performance from talk about raises or other compensation. _____

Given responses to above, do I clearly communicate expectations to my employees? _____

Average your ratings:

If average is 1: Outstanding performance that shows up in exceptional accomplishments of both you and your staff. You are an inspiration to direct reports.

If average is 2: Performance consistently meets and often exceeds requirements. Teamwork is usually accomplished in a highly effective way. You sometimes motivate employees.

If average is 3: Minimal expected. You get the job done.

If average is 4: Needs are being addressed inconsistently. Established requirements are not being met. Work tends to get done, but sometimes with less than complete effectiveness. Staff rarely receives recognition.

If average is 5: Performance is unacceptable. Established requirements are not being met.

Self-Assessment for Employees

How do you rate yourself on the following? (1 = very often; 5 = not at all)

Meet my yearly objectives. _____

Complete work assignments on time. _____

Make contributions to work group. _____

Work effectively with coworkers to accomplish department
goals. _____

Share important work information with others. _____

Talk to my supervisor when I need help. _____

Express interest in new challenges. _____

Make an effort to learn about my organization's goals and how
I can advance them. _____

Assist my boss without being asked. _____

Assist my coworkers without being asked. _____

Openly review my work to learn how I can improve. _____

Make an effort to build bridges with other departments. _____

Ask for feedback on several levels. _____

Average your ratings: _____

If average is 1: Outstanding performance that results in exceptional accomplishments. You are an extremely conscientious employee.

If average is 2: Performance consistently meets and frequently exceeds requirements. Work is accomplished in a highly effective manner.

If average is 3: Minimal expected level of performance. You are getting the job done.

If average is 4: Performance does not consistently meet established requirements. Duties and responsibilities are accomplished, but sometimes with less than complete effectiveness. Improvement is required. It would be wise to seek on-the-job guidance.

If average is 5: Performance is unacceptable and does not meet established requirements. Key responsibilities are not being fulfilled. Improved performance is necessary and must be sustained for successful employment. On-the-job guidance is vital.

Forget Winging It!

2

Understanding should precede judging.

—Louis D. Brandeis,
U.S. Supreme Court Justice,
1916 to 1939

Former New York Mayor Ed Koch did it directly. "How am I doing?" he'd ask, as he walked in parades, greeted visitors, and strolled Manhattan's streets. For the rest of us there's paperwork. Usually lots of it. A recurring complaint about performance appraisals is that "forms are endless and there's no guidance in using them."

Winging it isn't the answer. It almost guarantees morale, management and legal dilemmas, and the inconsistency from one department to another does nothing but impede an organization's mission and goals.

Given that performance appraisals are a fact of 21st century work life, and bound to come in widely diverse shapes and sizes that are most often handed to you, the best single way to deal with any of them is to be clear—*before* the appraisal—about whom you are evaluating, what you are evaluating, and why your appraisal is geared in one direction or another (the latter bolstered by a number of objective, legally sound examples). Henry

Ford said, "Before everything else, getting ready is the secret of success.[1] As a hallmark of effective performance management, performance appraisals rarely work well on the fly.

Preparedness on everyone's part marks the difference between an uninformed appraisal that's frustrating, futile, and possibly legally hazardous, and a performance appraisal that elevates shared understanding, communication and, within the framework of clear goals, achievements over the next appraisal cycle and beyond. What's really needed is a review before the review. A solid checklist that rather than add another layer to a possibly already undesired review will make the whole review process smoother, more productive, and legally defensible.

Some things to keep in mind:

Know Your Employee or Your Supervisor

If you're an employee whose supervisor doesn't often open the door, take the initiative to make an appointment to talk to him or her periodically. Angst comes when the performance review is really the single time, or just one of the very few times, that supervisors and employees sit down together during the year. One organization asked their employees to complete the appraisal form—in the third person! That turned out to be the actual form! Employees felt duped, believing their supervisors didn't care enough to even fill out the form. Optimally, a performance evaluation is a wrap-up of a series of informal discussions held throughout the year and a springboard from which to move forward, with new ideas, improved performance, and perhaps more responsibility.

Knowing a supervisor or employee means being better able to anticipate the reaction to your comments, and then "managing" your reaction to generate positive results. It's also, of course, highly useful to know yourself. Managers' effectiveness is significantly influenced by insight into their

Dilbert reprinted by permission of United Syndicate, Inc.

own work. Managers who can be introspective about their work are likely to be effective at their jobs.[2] The same applies to employees, who seek not just success but gratification. By its nature, self-gratification is self-defined.

Demonstrate Respect and Confidentiality

How, when, and even if appraisals are conducted send a strong message. When a supervisor delays appraisals, does them on the fly, allows phone or other interruptions, doesn't have paperwork complete, and generally doesn't demonstrate that the performance evaluation is a priority, an employee may feel that he or she isn't either. If an employee shows up late, only half-heartedly participates, takes no initiative in goal-setting, and sits waiting only for compensation information, you can bet the supervisor is similarly hearing a loud message. Respectful interaction during the appraisal reflects on the broader relationship and is a harbinger of the quality of day-to-day work life. Setting aside sufficient time in a private setting, with no interruption, is key. Confidentiality is, too. Only those with a need to know should be privy to the conversation and the form.

Don't Prejudge

Our first impressions of others take place automatically, and the prejudgment process goes on largely unnoticed by our conscious minds. Past experiences, needs and wishes, and assumptions about the context in which we encounter new people all greatly influence what information we attend to and how we interpret it. Research indicates that even after months of regular interaction, roughly two-thirds of our first impressions remain unchanged.[3] The hiring process alone does not give supervisors and employees the opportunity to know each other well, and upfront impressions can be frozen or misplaced unless there are continuing two-way avenues of feedback.

Keep Messages Clear and Direct

Know when something needs to be said; then, based on solid documented examples, make sure it is being relayed accurately. Never assume that supervisors or employees know what you think, want, or need. Not being direct can be costly. Hints are often misinterpreted or ignored. Keeping messages clear depends on awareness, knowing what you have observed, and knowing how you have reacted to it, especially because what we see and hear externally is so easily confused with what we think and feel inside.

Separating these elements will go a long way toward communicating clearly and directly.[4]

Keep Messages Straight

A straight message is one in which the stated purpose is identical with the real purpose of communication. Disguised intentions and hidden agendas are manipulative. Check whether your messages are straight by asking:

1. Why am I saying this to this person?

2. Do I want him or her to hear it, or something else?[5]

You'll know quickly whether the points you're highlighting need to be clarified, strengthened, or scrapped.

Review Job Description

For starters, make sure there is one—and that it's accurate and up-to-date. If not, one needs to be developed, with employee input. That should occur prior to the session so that the job description can be discussed and in place for the next performance cycle. Along with goals, the job description is a key basis for gauging performance effectiveness and whether organizational and departmental needs and supervisor and employee expectations are all on one track. Perhaps new responsibilities have been added over the review cycle, or there's interest in adding them. There may be recent team or work group initiatives that should be integrated. Perhaps there is a community liaison role that has not been acknowledged. Employees are the people most aware of on-the-job responsibilities that, despite being regularly addressed, are not in their job descriptions. The descriptions further serve to measure employee workloads and the need to develop new skills to best perform new tasks.

Track Performance Year-round

Have a handy folder to toss in quick notes, including positive observations, others' feedback, memos, award notices, and other items that reflect on performance evaluations. Create an e-mail file for the same purpose and periodically print out the e-mails and add them to the folder. It's important to think of this as an active folder, not one to dust off yearly. Use it as a basis for regular ongoing discussion. It may seem time-consuming, but it's much easier, more productive, and more fair than having to draw on memory once a year. An appraisal at the end of a given cycle works much better as a recap with recognition, or as an opportunity to stimulate improvement plans than it does as a surprise that is uncomfortable to both supervisors and employees. Being caught off guard serves only to tap into fears described in Chapter 1. Not having specific examples to support your ratings can lead to the legal problems noted in Chapter 9.

Stay Up-to-Date on Organizational Goals

Know what's going on in your organization. Effectively tying job description and goals to broader needs requires a good grasp on organizational direction and changes. Stay in touch with changes along the way, and be prepared to factor what is needed and/or desired into ongoing responsibilities. When information isn't shared by supervisors, misinformation flies freely and morale can plummet. Employees should feel comfortable asking questions and offering to pitch in on new initiatives even if supervisors rarely or never initiate discussion.

Consider the Ground Rules

If you're a supervisor, should there be any ground rules? Does your organization mandate any? If not, perhaps it should. Ground rules might cover ensuring two-way conversation, setting guidelines for goal-setting and problem-solving, applying techniques to stay on track, developing standards for addressing conflict, and delaying talk about compensation for a timely follow-up session. Each of these topics is considered in subsequent chapters but it's important to list them here because each will predictably come up in at least some if not all performance reviews. If you're an employee being appraised, the ground rules are more informal but nonetheless important—and up to you to implement. The most productive appraisals are clear, open two-way discussions. Honesty and clarity, bolstered by written examples, are fair expectations, but may require some added determination if your work climate does not readily invite openness.

Follow up Quickly with Compensation Discussion

Thoughts about compensation inevitably shadow the appraisal session. It's unrealistic to think otherwise. There is support for factoring discussion about pay right into the review. There is also strong advocacy for scheduling two discussions: the first about performance; the second about pay. This precludes tendency of employees to want to discuss examples of stellar performance and explain away anything that might negatively affect the increase. The meeting can turn into a battle of explanations between manager and employee rather than an open discussion of performance and how it can be improved.[6] When the compensation talk is scheduled separately, it should be held very soon after the performance appraisal, perhaps even at the end of that session.

■ ■ ■ ■ ■ ■ ■ ■ ■ ■

Preparation Pays Off...for Supervisors and Their Employees

Make sure to review the following:

- ◙ Strategic plan.

- ◙ Updated job description.

- ◙ Evaluation form/rating structure.

- ◙ Prior performance appraisal.

- ◙ Personnel file documentation.

- ◙ Goals for current review cycle.

- ◙ Preliminary appraisal recommendations—positive and/or negative aspects.

- ◙ Documented examples, including letters of praise and award information.

- ◙ As needed, suggestions for improvement, such as training, Performance Improvement Plan.

- ◙ List of questions.

- ◙ Anticipated reaction and how to best respond, if warranted.

■ ■ ■ ■ ■ ■ ■

Review Before the Review

Before the review, employers sometimes ask staff to complete the actual appraisal form, or to perform self-evaluations and/or appraise their supervisors. Other forms may seek feedback about development needs, training interests, ideas for new projects, and areas of concern. The responses may be viewed in advance or discussed for the first time during the review. It is also important that the supervisor's supervisor review the appraisal before it is shared with the employee. This provides built-in safeguards that can be significant to employees, supervisors, and organizations.

At a Mid-Atlantic country club, managers ask: "Will both the employee and I know when this goal has been achieved?" An international hotel chain develops appraisal forms designed specifically to particular jobs. A financial firm in Virginia has an optional employee preevaluation sheet that is reviewed by supervisors before the evaluation and attached to the evaluation form. Five questions probe: quality of performance against the performance plan, success in fostering customer satisfaction, team and work group contributions, challenges desired over the upcoming year, and the training needed to undertake them.

Many companies ask employees to be ready with a list of accomplishments. Even if not asked, it's an excellent idea to have them. As previously underscored, the importance of documenting is key for supervisors, too. *Not* doing it year-round can backfire. In one case, a supervisor realized that her employee was not contributing in the way he presented it in his preappraisal form. She wanted to place him on probation but, without her own supporting documentation, there was just his "record" of stellar performance. It was only then that the supervisor began documenting his poor performance. Chapter 9 examines the legal importance of solid documentation.

Smart companies do everything they can to give managers and employees a comfort level with the appraisal process. They underscore that it is part of the work process, and not an annual event. They circulate the appraisal form in advance so that features and ratings are clear. Many make it available on their Intranet. One association pulled together a panel of seasoned supervisors who talked about their own appraisal experiences and shared techniques that worked. Some organizations have a brown-bag lunch, show a video, and encourage discussion.

One company scheduled small group meetings so that supervisors who worked with certain employees could collectively share impressions of their work, giving more balance to each evaluation and fostering consistency in evaluations throughout the organization. Some organizations make sure that everyone—supervisors and employees alike—have copies of the strategic plan in hand prior to appraisal time, with plenty of time to review it. The expectation is that it dovetails with goal-setting. As a new appraisal cycle nears, some companies distribute articles to stimulate thinking about the process. Others pull together "asset lists" of training possibilities, videos, and other resources complementary to the appraisal process. And a few organizations make sure that supervisors don't receive their reviews until all staff reviews are completed first.

■ ■ ■ ■ ■ ■ ■ ■ ■ ■ ■ ■

Employee-driven "Max Plan"

National Cooperative Bank, a financial services company in Washington, DC, calls its appraisal process the Max Plan. At the start of each year, a memo to all employees outlines the goals of the performance appraisal process. What's unusual is that the entire process is employee-driven. Employees seek feedback from their managers and team members, then review their prior year's Max Plan and assess achievements demonstrating measurable results. They then draft a new plan—all before meeting with their supervisors. Inherent are the bank's values, including coaching/mentoring, supporting others' development, building trust, and aligning performance for success and teamwork.

▨ ▨ ▨ ▨ ▨ ▨ ▨

To steer preparation, it's helpful to answer three questions.[7] The responses can open many avenues of thinking. Employees can consider these questions in advance, and supervisors might suggest they do.

- ▣ What actions have you taken?

- ▣ What discoveries have you made?

- ▣ What partnerships have you built?

Increasingly, smaller businesses, associations, law firms, and other such organizations are recognizing the value of not merely conducting appraisals but of sound preparation. Many organizations conduct annual performance evaluation training. Whether managed internally or handled by a consultant, the training takes many forms. It may be just for supervisors, or for both supervisors and employees in mixed or separate sessions. Role plays often provide useful coaching for both. A labor lawyer might conduct training specific to legal issues. Training workshops track the entire process, from broadly clarifying why appraisals are so important, to self-assessment, goal-setting, and problem-solving exercises, to being tuned into rating errors. New software is making a difference. Some products allow the strategic plan and goals to be programmed. They also permit supervisors to type in employee ratings, yielding a clear, objective interpretation that helps a supervisor assess whether the rating really lines up with the intent. Seeing the write-up of a "poor rating," for example, may either bolster a supervisor's decision or trigger a change.

■ ■ ■ ■ ■ ■ ■ ■ ■ ■ ■ ■

Qualities of Successful Supervisor/Employee Partnerships

- ▣ Demonstrated mutual respect.

- ▣ Frequent, two-way communication.

- ▣ Shared contributions to a risk-free environment that invites healthy debate.

- ▣ Active listening.

- ▣ Mutual support.

- ▣ Both roll sleeves up in a crisis.

■ ■ ■ ■ ■ ■ ■

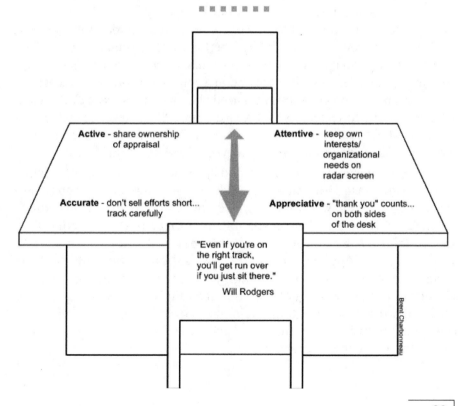

Active - share ownership of appraisal

Attentive - keep own interests/ organizational needs on radar screen

Accurate - don't sell efforts short... track carefully

Appreciative - "thank you" counts... on both sides of the desk

"Even if you're on the right track, you'll get run over if you just sit there."

Will Rodgers

Brent Charbonneau

The "A" List

As this book evolved, four qualities began to surface. Although appearing under many theories and with a wide diversity of names and labels, these qualities seemed to thread case studies, the extensive research of others, and interviews at all employment levels. They boil down to the recommendation that, throughout the year, both supervisors and employees would benefit from being active, accurate, attentive, and appreciative. However they are worded and framed, these qualities appear intrinsic in preparing for performance appraisals that represent a step-up in fostering excellent supervisor/ employee working relationships. All four can contribute to ease of communication between supervisor and employee year-round. While these qualities are not the measurable standards on which performance appraisals must be based, they are harbingers of positive on-the-job experiences and key aspects of effective supervisor and employee relationships.

Being active means sharing ownership of the appraisal. Make it count as a stepping stone. Active preparation, then enthusiastic engagement during the actual session, go a fair distance toward a supervisor's saying, "You matter," or an employee's communicating, "This work is important to me beyond a paycheck." Pride and accomplishment cannot be created outside of the job, and work but must grow out of them.[8] The performance appraisal is an excellent opportunity to wrap-up a series of informal discussions, assess goals set in the prior appraisal cycle, and move forward in a way that builds pride, recognizes accomplishment, sets new goals and, if needed, creates measurable clarity about what needs to be corrected. As Will Rodgers put it, "Even if you're on the right track, you'll get run over if you just sit there."[9] The performance appraisal represents a springboard for actively moving ahead on the right track.

Being accurate is similarly an indispensable dimension of performance appraisals. Documenting work performance is often challenging enough, even without opening the door to questions about accuracy. Because it's unreasonable to expect that all accomplishments, trip-ups, and other important appraisal information can be kept in sight throughout an entire appraisal cycle, particularly if the cycle is yearlong, there is a strong need for the continuing tracking. Recent initiatives will stay fresh, but accurately documenting the full scope of work takes ongoing vigilance. Good records can mark the difference between "meeting" or "exceeding" expectations or countering the evidence that a performance is below par.

Being attentive means keeping your goals on the radar screen. It requires staying abreast of changing organizational needs and structure, new project opportunities, increasing professional or personal stress on employee or supervisor, and other clues that can translate into changes in your work life. While not directly tied to performance appraisals, an understanding of such occurrences can help shape their outcome, especially if your attentiveness means initiating fresh responsibility, temporarily offering to pick up a project, or perhaps envisioning an added role for yourself or your department while organizational change is still conceptual.

Sir Arthur Conan Doyle's success in crafting Sherlock Holmes is "largely attributable to the fact that Holmes knew how to make the most of non-verbal communication." But Sir Arthur "only made explicit a highly complex process that many of us go through [without even knowing it]. Those of us who keep our eyes open can read volumes into what we see going on around us."[10]

Ideally, *being appreciative* would not need to be built in, but it often does need to be. In whatever form, periodic recognition—from both sides of the desk—clearly eases the review process. Comments such as, "I knew what was coming would be fair" and "there are no hidden agendas" came from employees whose supervisors took the time to praise good work, explain any concerns, and simply say thank you for extra effort. Supervisors appreciated "questions in advance instead of missed deadlines when something isn't clear," "being trusted enough to be asked for support," and a thank you for providing that support. "Employees increasingly believe that their job satisfaction depends on acknowledgment of work performance as well as on adequate salary,"[11] a finding that is widely reinforced. Compensation in its many forms is examined in Chapter 5.

■ ■ ■ ■ ■ ■ ■ ■ ■ ■ ■ ■

Styles at Work

This list provides a glimpse of the styles that shape daily worklife. Where do you fit? And how closely does that match the styles of your employees/supervisor/team members? There are excellent tools available to help carefully measure styles and provide insight into how various styles mesh in the workplace.

◙ Direct/ Indirect.

◙ Introverted/Extroverted.

- ◙ Crisis Mode/Balanced.

- ◙ Detailed/Unstructured.

- ◙ Intuitive/Analytical.

- ◙ Assertive/Passive.

- ◙ Ambitious/Content with Status Quo.

- ◙ Dependable/Undependable.

- ◙ Persistent /Lax.

- ◙ Dogmatic/ Open.

- ◙ Tense/Laid Back.

■ ■ ■ ■ ■ ■ ■

Three Scenarios

This book is about human interaction. For this reason we have factored in composites of actual people whom we'll call Marilyn, Richard, and Peg. You'll meet them and read their stories at various points throughout this book.

Marilyn, age 42, is office administrator of a medium-sized Chicago law firm. She is constantly busy, with broad responsibilities for personnel, budget, new equipment, file indexes, and occasional expansion of physical facilities. Marilyn is on the recruitment team for associate lawyers and coordinator of the annual attorney retreat. She is an excellent employee who manages her time efficiently. She is well compensated and feels highly appreciated by both attorneys and support staff. Frequently approached by competing firms, Marilyn is a much sought after administrator. The challenge is to keep her satisfied and motivated.

To prepare for her performance appraisal, Marilyn can:

- ▣ Track her workload.

- ▣ Compare her present responsibilities with last year's job description, listing added responsibilities.

- ▣ List accomplishments in the present review cycle.

- ▣ Underscore how she may have leveraged accomplishments.

▣ Envision what more she would like to do, including any training required to do it.

▣ Draw on her excellent track record, clear value to her firm, and understanding of personnel parameters to seek what she most wants.

▣ Prepare a back-up plan just in case.

Marilyn's supervisor can:

▣ Review her job description.

▣ Plan to recognize her terrific work, value to the firm, and continuing loyalty.

▣ Plan to acknowledge that she's in high demand.

▣ Set aside sufficient time to thoroughly listen to and discuss her ideas and proposals.

▣ Prepare new challenges to keep her motivated.

Richard, age 36, is a duplicating supervisor in charge of overseeing the day-to-day operations of his department. He interviews and hires staff and ensures that they are well trained from the start. He assigns jobs to technicians, keeps tabs on new technology, verifies and approves time sheets, and makes sure that all duplicating requests are fulfilled quickly and efficiently. Richard used to excel on the job. Right now he's constantly distracted by concern for a parent who is slowly recovering after serious illness. His parent lives alone and Richard is often called upon for help. The challenge is to support his present needs, yet make sure he again meets his responsibilities in an outstanding manner.

To prepare for his performance appraisal, Richard can:

▣ Track his workload.

▣ Compare his present responsibilities with last year's job description.

▣ List added responsibilities.

▣ List accomplishments, if any, in the present review cycle.

▣ Prepare how to acknowledge shortcomings resulting from parent's illness.

◙ Prepare a plan to help support current, possibly long-term situation.

◙ Recommit to focusing more effectively at work.

Richard's supervisor can:

◙ Review job description.

◙ Prepare to acknowledge a difficult situation.

◙ Prepare a list of mounting concerns but also some positives.

◙ Plan how to again engage and refocus Richard, seeking his suggestions in advance so that review will have a more upbeat tone—Richard is bound to be dreading this review.

◙ Plan to set measurable goals for improvement, along with a time frame for assessing their delivery.

◙ Prepare information regarding Employee Assistance Program and other resources that can help Richard.

Peg, age 27, is receptionist for an advertising agency. She greets clients, maintains security in the reception area, handles the switchboard, tracks comings and goings of employees, sets up client files, lines up equipment for meetings, and picks up secretaries' typing overloads. Peg is a poor performer. She is often late, takes unscheduled days off, does not consistently get deliveries out on time, and often errs in taking messages and other administrative duties. Despite several coaching sessions, some adjustment of her hours to accommodate travel time, monitoring to be sure her workload isn't excessive, and many reminders, Peg has shown little improvement. She's now in job-jeopardy, with a written warning in her personnel file. The challenge is to put her on a Performance Improvement Plan (Chapter 8) and give her one last chance.

To prepare for her performance appraisal, Peg can:

◙ Determine whether she values her job and wants to keep it.

◙ Review the warning in her personnel file, review her job description and workload.

◙ Prepare a list of solutions to documented problems and clear time lines for delivery.

Peg's supervisor can:

- ▣ Review her job description.

- ▣ Review documented discussions and warnings.

- ▣ Document performance since most recent warning.

- ▣ Plan to discuss continuing commitment to work with her, identifying training.

- ▣ Develop a Performance Improvement Plan.

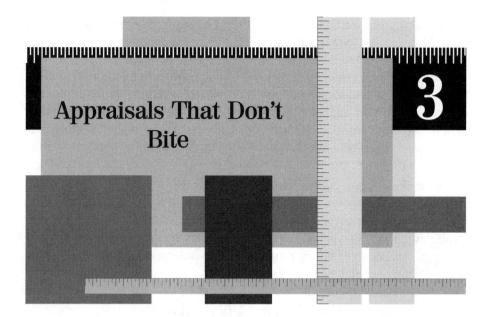

Appraisals That Don't Bite

3

Organizations...are not paying enough attention to doing the right thing, while paying too much attention to doing things right.

> —Warren Bennis, former university
> president, presidential adviser,
> and leadership guru.

Too often, the evaluation form predominates. Instead of supporting the appraisal, it becomes the centerpiece, functioning as a hurdle to just get through until the next deadline comes up. A bank vice president reflected the thoughts of several interviewees when she said that "completing the form feels as if the appraisal is all done." Another manager perceived an unfriendly roadmap, saying, "evaluation forms leave lots of room for the negatives and just a few lines for the positive stuff." Perhaps this isn't surprising. "Betraying their partial origin from the study of clinical psychology, many performance appraisals often seek out weaknesses rather than pointing out strengths [even though] individuals are employed for what they can do, not for what they cannot do."[1]

A survey of Fortune 500 companies showed that only about 10 percent of employees were satisfied with their organization's performance evaluation methods.[2] A survey by Mercer Human Resource Consulting found that 78 percent of companies routinely conduct annual performance reviews and communicate the results to workers. But only 26 percent of employees said managers routinely provide constructive feedback and/or coaching. It's no wonder that Mercer's Colleen O'Neill said, "Performance evaluations are often viewed as something that those at the top tell the middle to do to the bottom." [3]

What lost opportunities! Organizations invest untold millions in fostering motivated employees and many millions more to keep that motivation alive. Yet the performance appraisal, which, in one form or another, is probably going to occur at least annually anyway, is too infrequently valued as a vital contributor to performance management.

■ ■ ■ ■ ■ ■ ■ ■ ■ ■ ■ ■ ■

No Longer "A Black Box"

At SC Johnson, a multinational company run by the same family for more than 117 years, the performance management process used to be seen as "a black box." Employees weren't sure how data went in and performance ratings and merit dollars came out. But the Wisconsin-based company turned things around, creating communications tools and training around a new Performance Management Process. Employees now understand how data turn into ratings, dollars, and feedback that is used to coach and develop improved performance.

The Performance Management Process lines up objective-setting, ongoing feedback and coaching, performance review, and career development planning. Responsibilities are shared. The company offers development opportunities so that employees can grow in current jobs, prepare for greater responsibilities, and enjoy personal growth. Managers help employees understand what their performance standards are, how they're doing relative to these standards, what development may be needed, and which opportunities can be beneficial. Employees are expected to maintain effective performance, initiate growth opportunities, and manage the progression of their own careers.

■ ■ ■ ■ ■ ■ ■

Tapping Into Motivation

"Motivation is what impels us to do certain things rather than others; to wish for certain things rather than others; to react to persons and situations in a manner peculiar to ourselves."[4] In other words, motivation is personal. The performance review must be, too. Each review is a highly individual matter. What makes an employee want to excel? How can an employee best communicate his or her personal best to a supervisor? Tapping into motivation requires preparedness, understanding, sound listening skills, and a supportive work climate. Above all, it requires a willingness to genuinely know the person you're facing. A once-a-year review won't do it. If performance feedback is not ongoing, the appraisal can happen almost by rote, reminiscent of the way journalist Edwin Newman's wry eye viewed the World Series: "with play determined not by the quality of the teams but by the annual occurrence of October."[5] With appraisals, of course, both sides can emerge as winners.

Motivated individuals will seek to do that. Maslow's "Hierarchy of Needs" theory explained that, when not blocked, people will move up a ladder of needs to fulfill their potential. Satisfying one need sets the stage for advancing to the next. In this chain of needs, Maslow placed "esteem" as fourth, before self-actualization, and after the satisfaction of physiological, safety, and social needs. "Individuals are motivated by the esteem they hold for themselves and in which they are held by others. Although real achievements are rewards in themselves, there is much enjoyment from the recognition and respect of others."[6] Published in 1959, the work of psychologist Frederick Herzberg is often cited as empirical evidence supportive of Maslow's needs' theory.[7] In focusing on reasons for job satisfaction and dissatisfaction, Herzberg, too, identified recognition as being among the positive factors. Among his principles for implementing job enrichment, Herzberg underscored "increased accountability, feedback, and providing new learning experiences"[8] as being fixtures of most sound performance reviews. Herzberg's research showed that linking work and personal satisfaction is a potent motivator.

What does it take to move performance evaluations in a posistive direction? First, there is the review before the review. Then, there is a careful, motivating appraisal discussion. Both supervisor and employee are key to the productivity of this discussion, which merits private, sufficient, and uninterrupted time. The clear message is: performance reviews are important because both employees and their organizational contributions are important. Conducting a respectful review drives this message home.

Just as with compensation systems, most managers and their employees inherit both the appraisal process and the paperwork that reflects it. As a result, this chapter focusses on the conversation that should be requisite to all appraisals rather than tackling appraisal forms themselves. Sometimes positive appraisal experiences can be leveraged to shake things up a bit so that entire organizations benefit. To generate more two-way feedback, managers may also have the flexibility to create an "add-on" to the organization's form, such as the one developed by an association director that appears on pages 63 and 64. This form worked well in complementing the association's long-standing standard form, which was basically a lengthy checklist.

If you're a supervisor headed into appraisal discussions, it's useful to remember that your best assets go home at night. Successful change depends on individual people and their collective actions. "By showing trust in and respect for all employees, managers can empower people to do their jobs to the very best of their ability. As Martin Marietta's former president, Tom Young, liked to observe, 'No one shows up in the morning thinking: I guess I'll see how badly I can mess up today, but an unenlightened management can put them in that frame of mind by 9 a.m.' By cultivating and investing time in employees, managers strengthen the foundation of the entire enterprise."[9]

As the employee being appraised, you might take inventory. Who you are determines what you see. Do you see a solution in every challenge, or a problem in every circumstance? When it comes to approaching problems, are you likely to flee them, fight them, forget them, or face them? It may be necessary to get out of the box of your typical thinking.[10]

"Both supervisors and employees can reap rewards by breaking the Golden Rule. Following it presupposes that everyone breathes the same psychological oxygen,"[11] which is rarely the case. Before the discussion, be very clear about what you value, what your supervisor or employee values, what your organization values, and the documentation vital to supporting these perspectives. Bring along the four As of positive on-the-job experiences referenced in Chapter 2—being active, accurate, attentive, and appreciative—and you're set to open the discussion.

■ ■ ■ ■ ■ ■ ■ ■ ■ ■ ■ ■

Four Season's Job-specific Forms

Believing that job-specific appraisal forms are the most accurate method of assessing performance, Four Seasons Hotels and Resorts has created Employee and Management Development Reviews. Designed to foster positive, productive relationships between supervisors and employees, these reviews are tailored to make sure that employees know what is expected of them and how well these expectations are being met. The reviews help ensure that pay is related to work performance and that there is equal pay for equal work. They motivate employees to maintain or improve high performance levels and provide the basis for development plans and promotion and salary decisions.

Underscoring confidence and self-esteem as trademarks of effective employees, Four Seasons advocates positive feedback from management and co-workers and, as part of the appraisal process, regular, clear, honest feedback on performance against expected standards based on adequate observation. Aimed at an exchange of expectations leading to a shared understanding of goals, Four Seasons requests that evaluations occur as often as necessary, but at least annually. Emphasis is put on rating performance only and leaving the rating of "potential" to a Management Development Planning process. When necessary, an Individual Development Plan highlighting training needs is designed for an employee after the performance appraisal is completed.

■ ■ ■ ■ ■ ■ ■

■ ■ ■ ■ ■ ■ ■ ■ ■ ■ ■ ■

Motivational Benchmarks

- ▣ Clear, challenging goals.

- ▣ Good working conditions.

- ▣ Reliable, helpful team members.

- ▣ Effective communication from higher up.

- ▣ Ongoing feedback from boss and others.

- ▣ Consistently applied policies and procedures.

- ▣ A certain amount of autonomy.

- ▣ Recognition for a job well-done.

■ ■ ■ ■ ■ ■ ■

Upbeat Openings

In opening the discussion, supervisors might recall their own feelings about being evaluated. Empathy can spur an approach, tone, and even body language that makes the entire meeting much more friendly. Supervisors can realize that employees not only want feedback but have a right to it. Employees want to know how they're doing, whether expectations are on track, and what the future holds. Employees seek recognition and rewards. Supervisors want the satisfaction of a management function well-done. If this discussion is the culmination of a number of mini-meetings, or series of quick or lengthy two-way talks about performance feedback, there should be no surprises. One national financial institution uses a form that tracks goals throughout the entire performance cycle. Supervisors and employees meet at least quarterly and both can gauge progress at any point along the way.

Usually evaluations are not as frequent and sometimes it is helpful for either the supervisor and/or employee to acknowledge upfront that the appraisal discussion is a bit uncomfortable or anxiety provoking. As necessary, it provides the opening to reassure employees that the review contains many positive aspects. The supervisor can also underscore his or her interest in the employee's growth and development. Be clear that the goal is to summarize what has already been shared at mini-meetings and then to move on from there.

A brief warm-up can set a comfortable tone. While this is a professional meeting and small talk should be minimal, employees (and supervisors) must also be relaxed enough to become genuinely engaged. The aim is to be open, friendly, and positive. Both supervisors and employees can demonstrate interest in trading views and discussing particular projects or aspects of performance. The climate should be inviting and non-threatening, with both supervisors and employees open to hearing concerns without getting defensive. Supervisors might heed U.S. Secretary of State Colin Powell's words: "The day soldiers stop bringing you their problems is the day you have stopped leading them."[12]

Employees need time to really read what their supervisors are saying. If they can't review the appraisal prior to the meeting, sufficient time is needed early in the discussion. Supervisors may wish to step out of the office for a while so that employees can better focus. It's important for supervisors to reassure employees that the appraisal is confidential and will not be left where others can read it.

Then, the supervisor and his or her employee can review the appraisal form jointly and identify points of agreement or disagreement. If there is a self-appraisal, the supervisor and employee can go back and forth between the appraisal and self-appraisal forms throughout the meeting. Be ready to ask for examples and give examples for any areas of disagreement.

Supervisors can kick off the discussion with such open-ended questions as:

- How do you think things have been going?

- Do my ratings seem fair? Then, why or why not?

- Would you have done anything differently this year?

If an employee isn't ready or willing to participate, the supervisor can consider postponing the meeting, explaining that it won't be productive unless the employee actively participates. Emphasize that discussion is two-way. Considerable participation by and input from the employee is important for the employee's perception that the process is fair.[13] Setting ground rules upfront can help, such as by stating, "I look forward to hearing from you about 60 percent of the time."

■ ■ ■ ■ ■ ■ ■ ■ ■ ■ ■ ■

Ice Breakers

For Supervisors

- What suggestions do you have on meeting next year's goals?

- What changes/refinements would you suggest?

- What's your point of view?

- What would you like to work on?

- How can I best help you during the coming year?

For Employees

- How do you see my skills best fitting organizational needs?

- What's your reaction to [cite specific initiative]?

- What do you see as the next steps in my development?

- How can I better support you and this department?

- What do you see as my three key priorities in the months ahead?

Employee-driven Objectives

At the National Health Service Hospital in the UK, where supervisors and employees jointly set work objectives, employees reported finding the process beneficial as long as they were actively engaged in the process. They reported that the objectives they set for themselves were more interesting and challenging than those set by their supervisors. Employees also reported pursuing growth opportunities through the objective-setting process. Because the hospital encourages mini-reviews throughout the year, the annual reviews are mainly a confirmation of these agreements, allowing a focused look at objectives for the coming cycle.[14]

Building Productive Discussions

In most discussions, there are two parties. There are also two equally important actions—*talking* and *listening*. One doesn't work well without the other. Other factors may also frame the appraisal discussion. The prior experiences of one or both parties may crowd the room. There might also be powerful resistance to self-disclosure, even societal bias. It may not be considered "nice" to discuss true feelings beyond a narrow family circle. There may be concerns about rejection or punishment, or that revealing something positive will be received as bragging. Taking a stand means you may have to do something about it. There may also be fear of self-knowledge. You instinctively know that by disclosing yourself, you will come to know yourself better.[15]

While shared feelings are the building blocks of intimacy, the most difficult part of communication may be sharing these feelings. Some people don't want to hear what you feel. Some people are selectively receptive. Anger is the most discouraged feeling because it is threatening to the listener's self-esteem. Yet how you feel is a large part of what makes you unique and special.[16]

These feelings don't change simply because you're at work. At a basic level, the routes you choose for addressing your feelings probably don't change either. While it's important to be yourself, both in and out of work, reality checks about how you're doing can be reassuring. No matter how excellent the intent, any approach will go astray if it's moving in the wrong direction. Staying tuned in by seeking or providing feedback allows for a course correction. And *just hearing* that you're right on target is a good motivator. Clarity about how you're doing should be reinforced during the appraisal discussion—it should not be a *new* discovery.

Listening fully and openly are also hallmarks of productive reviews. Yogi Berra reportedly said, "You can observe a lot just by watching." The same applies to listening. There's a major difference between listening and hearing. Listening is active. Hearing is passive. Kicking off the appraisal discussion with open-ended questions will fall short if listening is not active. Information gained might contribute to a fairer rating. Terrific ideas and clues flagging serious concerns might be picked up as well. Vital bonds of shared understanding can be bolstered or doused depending on the quality of listening.

■ ■ ■ ■ ■ ■ ■ ■ ■ ■ ■ ■ ■

Active Listening

Aristotle counseled that we should use our two ears and one mouth proportionately. If we're committed to listening actively rather than merely hearing, that's an important skill to practice. Wendi Eldh, a corporate trainer in Albuquerque, refers to active listening as a contact sport. She developed the following guidelines for getting it right:

◙ Be prepared to listen. Handle current or possible distractions before the conversation begins. Turn cell phones and pagers off before the discussion starts.

◙ Focus on the speaker's words and body language. This means turning off internal distractions, too. Without staring, try to absorb the full message—it's physical, emotional, and verbal.

◙ Consider your own body language. Does it indicate your level of listening? Is your level of openness in tune with the speaker's? The speaker may be watching for physical clues that you are listening, especially if his or her body language is open. A muted and closed expression may convey a sense of your disapproval or disagreement.

◉ Open body language might include eye contact, relaxed open arms, and nods affirming certain points. Closed body language might include folded arms, shoulders or legs turned away, and quick willingness to focus on distractions.

◉ Provide verbal cues that you are being attentive. Periodically say, "yes," or "I see," or "I understand," to reinforce that you are listening.

◉ Most importantly, use feedback and questions to clarify meaning. Paraphrase the speaker's message to be certain you have understood. This both reduces ambiguity and emphasizes that you are listening. As needed, this will also help you replace old habits of merely hearing with active new ones of engagement.

■ ■ ■ ■ ■ ■ ■

Supervisors often build the appraisal discussion by reviewing significant accomplishments—giving praise and credit for quality work. When genuinely deserved, employees appreciate this praise and report finding it stimulating and motivating. Managers often begin with the strengths:

◉ *This year, you made important contributions in developing and administering our media strategies. On [dates], you were an effective spokesperson with the national and local press, and then on [date] you did an excellent job in explaining our initiatives to constituents.*

◉ *I'm impressed by the research you carried out this year. You developed an effective research design and data collection and analyses strategy. Because of your work, we'll be developing two new products.*

◉ *You've been more conscientious this year about managing the pension plan, processing 20 applicant loans and preparing 11 reports and information for the IRS audit.*

Supervisors generally work their way through each section of the form, focusing on technical aspects, then interpersonal ones. Objective measures are combined with soft skills. "What" was done and "how" the employee did it cover both bases. Statements and, as applicable, ratings should be documented by real work examples.

■■■■■■■■■■■■

What Works at GM?

"Is this a meaningful measure, and what element am I looking for in it?" Dennis Dreyer, director of logistics for service parts operations at General Motors, said that's the first question asked when developing measures. For measures to work for employees, GM believes four areas must be clear: data must be timely (available monthly, weekly, or daily); measures must be written in terms understood by users (financial measures for finance staff, etc.); measures must be sufficiently detailed; and employees need to be clear about which issues the measures support. Does a measure pertain to strategic, operational, or tactical issues?[17]

■ ■ ■ ■ ■ ■ ■

Beyond the Comfort Zone

After commenting on strengths, it may be necessary to consider where performance fell short. Documentation is key. Although many managers report this part is outside of their comfort zone, the reasons for substandard performance must be explored. The problem might not even lie with the employee, but with a process or other cause.

The following example shows how a supervisor stepped up to the plate, recognizing an employee's achievements yet candidly expressing, in a supportive way, exactly where improvement is required:

Doug, as project manager, you brought in that technology project on time and under budget. You used excellent planning and implementing skills. As we discussed when it happened, I observed that, at times, you weren't responsive when other task force members questioned a decision. At one point, you agreed to a suggested change but didn't interact with the team for the rest of the day. You bring a number of good skills to your assignments. However, this organization also values true collaboration and team spirit. You need to consistently interact with other team members in a way that makes them want to work on more projects with you. When team members make a suggestion, work with them to determine the usefulness of the suggestion. Express appreciation if it's an idea that will add value, or for suggesting it even if it's not. I would like you to be more proactive in eliciting ideas from the group.

Why don't you think about building in a brainstorming session during the planning phase? By taking this positive approach, you empower the team and it might result in a quicker turnaround on the project. That quality is necessary for a "fit" here. I would be remiss if I didn't bring this sensitive topic up. I want you to be successful here. You are an important member of the team. I have more ideas on how you can work on this. Why don't you attend one of my task force meetings, so you'll be able to see what I mean in action.

What are your ideas on how you can work on this?

Supervisors need to be direct about the type of behaviors they want to see. Employees should feel empowered to ask about their performance. Both should be open to sharing a candid discussion designed to turn a below-par performance around. In the previous example, Doug could have walked away from his appraisal thinking everything was great, or with the nagging feeling that he needed to improve without knowing how.

■ ■ ■ ■ ■ ■ ■ ■ ■ ■ ■ ■

Feedback Sandwich

When feedback is especially tough, and employees might react negatively, one HR manager advocates using a "feedback sandwich." Based on the understanding that "feedback" covers what one party needs, what the other party needs, and what the organization needs, the feedback sandwich is a six-step method for approaching a difficult discussion.

- ◼ The supervisor opens the discussion with a positive aspect of the employee's performance.

- ◼ The problem is identified and the supervisor explains his or her concerns.

- ◼ The employee is asked to explain his or her perspective.

◼ With examples, the supervisor outlines the effects of the behavior/action/lack of action on organizational goals.

◼ The employee is asked for solutions and, together, the supervisor and employee develop an action plan.

◼ The supervisor ends on an upbeat note, expressing confidence in the employee's capability to pursue a positive course.

▪ ▪ ▪ ▪ ▪ ▪ ▪

Make appraisals constructive, specific, and focused on performance, not personality:

Vague	Specific
You are often late.	You arrived 15-30 minutes after the start of your shift four times this month.
You seem to make a lot of errors.	During November, you made six errors on the monthly report, three errors on the customer letter, and routed five calls incorrectly.
You are never at your desk.	I went by your office four different times yesterday and you weren't there.

Stay calm. Be encouraging. If you're the supervisor, never discuss need for improvement in a way that is harsh. When valid, acknowledge the circumstances that were beyond the employee's control. Work for understanding rather than complete agreement. Aim for balance and to turn things around. Be ready to offer help. Clarify what needs to happen by identifying specific actions that employees can take. Refer to resources identified before the meeting for direction. Perhaps there's a helpful training class, or a book or mentor. Prepare a plan. Work for an agreement. Most importantly, express confidence that you can work through the issues together. Continue to check for reactions and understanding throughout the discussion. If you're the employee, be prepared with your own suggestions for improving performance and willingly participate in shaping a plan with clear benchmarks for marking improving performance.

■ ■ ■ ■ ■ ■ ■ ■ ■ ■ ■ ■

Killer Phrases

▣ That will never work.

▣ This is the way we'll do it.

▣ I know what's best.

▣ There's no money so why bother talking about it?

▣ Where's the logic?

▣ Why would you ever suggest something like that?

■ ■ ■ ■ ■ ■ ■

Targeting Objectives

Next is a critical phase of the appraisal discussion, in one sense the heart of the review. This phase involves the writing of objectives or targets for the following cycle. Vision Service Plan, the nation's largest provider of eyecare coverage and one of Fortune's "100 Best Companies To Work For" for four consecutive years, calls these objectives "key job accountabilities" or KJAs. The company believes these KJAs are key to the job, helping to identify the most important employee skills and values. The KJAs include specific performance measures, such as quantity, quality, and deadlines, and performance methods, such as teamwork, initiative, and leadership. Roger Valine, president and CEO, believes that honesty is a critical factor in quality reviews. He points out that appraisals at his company are a two-way street. "Supervisors shouldn't sugarcoat what isn't good. They are also encouraged to ask what they can do to be better supervisors."

■ ■ ■ ■ ■ ■ ■ ■ ■ ■ ■ ■

Objectives That Work

☑ Begin with an action verb.

☑ Specify, in writing, what needs to be accomplished.

☑ Clearly define how accomplishments are to be measured.

☑ Identify an end date.

☑ Link employee talents and organizational interests.

Example 1:

Design and conduct three supervisory skills modules: the first by October 10; the second by January 10; the third by April 10. On the post-test, everyone you have trained should achieve a score of 85 percent or higher. As the trainer, you should receive a 90 percent or higher approval rate from the participants on your delivery style and effectiveness.

Example 2:

Utilize various recruitment strategies to increase the number of 25- to 35-year-old members by 15 percent by 2005. Recruitment strategies must include elements of the following: direct mail, community membership drives, Internet and local broadcast and print media.

■ ■ ■ ■ ■ ■ ■

The joint process of writing objectives clarifies and directs behavior, providing employees with results-oriented challenges. Involved employees share ownership and pride of outcome rather than feeling as if objectives are being imposed on them. Whenever possible, objectives can be built around what employees most want to do. Motivated employees can make a pitch for the work they want, especially by underscoring organizational benefits. Objectives must be doable within given time frames and include clear performance standards. Without performance standards, how can a supervisor and employee know that their objectives have been reached?

Performance standards work as yardsticks in measuring employee performance.They usually measure either quality or productivity. A quality standard would require a salesman to close ten sales in three months without any errors in processing. A productivity standard would require a salesman to close ten sales in three months. When standards are clear and in writing, it's more difficult to disagree about the success of the accomplishment.

Sample measurement indicators include the following:[18]

1. **Quantity**

   ▪ Number of clients served per day.

   ▪ Number of items processed per week.

   ▪ Number of complaints handled per month.

2. **Quality**

   ▪ Error rate/ratio.

   ▪ Percentage of orders without errors.

   ▪ Percentage of work redone.

3. **Time**

   ▪ Number or percentage of deadlines missed.

   ▪ Number of calls answered within three rings.

   ▪ Turnaround time.

4. **Cost**

   ▪ Percent of variance from budget.

   ▪ Dollars saved over period.

   ▪ Overtime costs.

Objectives can reflect basic job duties, special responsibilities for particular projects, and organizational and departmental goals. Developmental areas for employees' growth are another important source of objectives. What can best help employees improve performance, move ahead, or fulfill their particular interests tied to organizational needs? Discuss any obstacles, such as time constraints and availability of resources.

■■■■■■■■■■■■

Weighing Objectives

Consider weighing, then prioritizing objectives based on importance. Supervisors and employees can do this together, factoring in the following variables:

- ▣ Impact on mission and strategic plan.

- ▣ Effort involved.

- ▣ Special knowledge or creativity required.

- ▣ Scope of project.

- ▣ Effect on other work.

- ▣ Repercussion of not achieving the objective.

■ ■ ■ ■ ■ ■ ■

Agree on a plan and commit it to paper. Make clear that the employee will be accountable for following through, and that the supervisor will monitor progress, provide guidance, and be available for occasional collaboration.

Three Scenarios

Markedly different objectives highlight the appraisals of Marilyn, Richard, and Peg, the composite people introduced in Chapter 2. Because she is already a terrific achiever, the challenge with Marilyn is to keep her enthusiasm high and engage her in identifying fresh goals to pursue in the year ahead. Recognizing how she enjoys developing programs and administering details, Marilyn's supervisor acknowledges her value to the firm, then suggests she take on the planning for her law firm's partner retreat for the coming year. Marilyn is asked to survey the firm's partners about topic choices, draft an agenda, suggest speakers, and present options and a budget to the planning committee within 10 weeks. Her already considerable day-to-day responsibilities of keeping the law firm running smoothly are also updated and spelled out on her appraisal, each with measurable goals. Given her enthusiastic approach to implementing numerous tasks, Marilyn and her supervisor schedule a mini-review in four weeks to be sure she's not too overloaded to meet expected deadlines.

Richard's situation is much different. Distracted by serious family illness, he's a good worker whose performance is sliding along with the situation. The challenge is to prevent further sliding and help renew Richard's pride in performing well. During the appraisal discussion, Richard's supervisor can acknowledge the difficulty of the situation and pass along the Employee Assistance Program information she obtained for him while preparing for the review. Because of Richard's excellent contributions to developing his company's Winter Technical Exhibit three years before, his supervisor works to engage him in the upcoming exhibit, not asking him to leave home to attend but, instead, partially delegating the responsibility of determining which of four senior copy technicians will represent their company. This will involve objectively discussing the qualifications of all technicians with their respective supervisors as part of the exhibit planning team, contributing to a written report, and helping to prepare the designated technician to attend, including providing input for a panel discussion and computer demonstration. This work all needs to be effectively concluded by the exhibit's opening in two months. Goals for Richard's daily responsibilities are set as well. The supervisor closes by acknowledging the tough circumstances and reinforcing that she has full confidence in Richard's commitment to meet his responsibilities. A mini-review is scheduled in three weeks to monitor Richard's work.

Despite continuing support, Peg's performance continues to be poor. But rather than turn the appraisal session into a termination, her supervisor again explains the concerns about Peg's performance and its adverse impact on the organization. The supervisor also tries to have Peg acknowledge her behavior. As a last effort to find a solution, the supervisor wants to schedule a meeting the following week to discuss a full Performance Improvement Plan. Peg agrees, realizing this is the last step.

■ ■ ■ ■ ■ ■ ■ ■ ■ ■ ■ ■

Evaluating Quantifiable Results

Dan Hague, president of three sports centers near Washington, DC, evaluates his employees on quantifiable results. His appraisal form is designed to measure a series of goals tied to membership numbers, bi-annual customer service ratings, and revenue generated by classes and equipment. That objective portion of the form yields 90 percent of the total score. The financial perspective portion of his form, for example, compares actual and budgeted sums for June and December. A budget off target by more than 10 percent is unacceptable. The customer perspective portion looks at customer satisfaction average scores of 80 percent or higher. Anything below 80 percent is unacceptable.

■ ■ ■ ■ ■ ■ ■

Successful Closes

As with the opening, aim for an upbeat close that paves the way for a mini-review in the near future. Before closing, supervisors can be sure that the job description is up-to-date. Employees can use this opportunity to suggest building in newly desired challenges. For both supervisors and their employees, it's a good time to ask whether the current workload makes sense. As an employee, do you feel overwhelmed or underwhelmed? As a supervisor, do you know how your employees would answer?

Before closing, managers might invite feedback about their own performance, or review a form similar to the one provided for such assessment at the end of this chapter. Asking what employees need from supervisors can yield a helpful blueprint for managerial efforts in the year ahead. As a supervisor, this blueprint could be a handy asset to bring to your own appraisal.

Summarizing what has been discussed is a productive way to close. To check for understanding, supervisors can ask employees to handle the summary. Supervisors and employees might also share thoughts about what was learned, whether there were any surprises, if there's a concern about balance, and general reactions. Employees can know that the door is always open if there's a delayed reaction to anything on the appraisal. They can also respond in writing.

Close on a friendly note. Supervisors can reinforce that the employee is part of an important team and that their performance counts. They can make clear that the discussion is about business and the employee, too. Employees can be appreciative of their supervisor's support and willingness to help guide their talents and interests right along with those of the organization. Appreciation can be expressed on both sides.

Employees sign and date the appraisal form with the understanding that this merely indicates that the form has been discussed. The employee should leave with a copy of the form. Confidentiality can again be stressed. It's up to the supervisor to make sure any promised follow-up occurs as quickly as feasible. It's up to the employee to initiate feedback about any areas of particular concern, especially if the supervisor is likely to bring them up at the next mini-review. It's also up to employees to keep supervisors informed about any work results.

■ ■ ■ ■ ■ ■ ■ ■ ■ ■ ■ ■ ■

Types of Appraisals

Performance can be recorded in many forms, including online.

Management by Objectives

Supervisors and employees set objectives together, defining what will be achieved within a specific time period. Objectives reflect organizational goals and objectives.

Absolute Standard or Category Rating

This is a single form recording method.

Graphic Scale Appraisal

Also known as the Adjective Rating Scale, this is one of the oldest and most popular methods. As the following shown, this method is used to assess dimension/performance factors. The appraiser marks points on the scale that best describe the employee. Generally, there is a "comments" section so the specifics can support the rating.

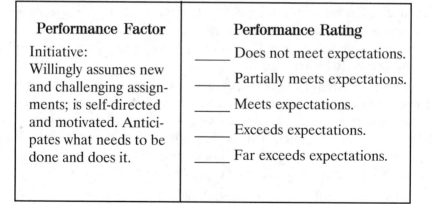

Performance Factor	Performance Rating
Initiative: Willingly assumes new and challenging assignments; is self-directed and motivated. Anticipates what needs to be done and does it.	_____ Does not meet expectations. _____ Partially meets expectations. _____ Meets expectations. _____ Exceeds expectations. _____ Far exceeds expectations.

Checklist Appraisal

On this form, the supervisor responds to the list of behavioral descriptions. Sometimes items are weighted to reflect importance.

Does the HR Assistant:	Yes	No
1. Post job ads on time?	❏	❏
2. Prepare complete orientation packets?	❏	❏
3. Maintain files accurately?	❏	❏
4. Answer employee questions promptly?	❏	❏
5. Computerize data promptly?	❏	❏
6. Support other staff as requested?	❏	❏

Forced-choice Appraisal

Choosing between two or more specific statements, the supervisor selects one that best describes the employee. In a variation of this form, the appraiser selects a statement that is "most like" the employee and another that is "least like."

Relative Standards or Comparative Ratings

These compare employees against other employees.

Group Order Ranking

Using this method, the supervisor must rank all employees that report to him/her in a particular classification, such as the top one-third.

Individual Ranking

Employees are ranked according to their work performance, from highest to lowest. There can be no ties.

Paired Comparison

Comparing each employee with every other member of the group, this method ranks employees' performances by counting the number of times any one individual is the highest/most-preferred when compared to the other employees.

Narratives

These provide a written assessment as opposed to a checklist.

Essay Appraisal

As long or short as a supervisor desires, the essay describes employee strengths, areas for development, achievement of goals, plans for development, etc.

Critical Incident Appraisal

Focused on key behaviors that define aspects of the job, the supervisor details specific, work-related anecdotes conveying what an employee did or didn't do.

Behaviorally Anchored Rating Scales

Coupling elements from the Critical Incident and Adjective Rating Scale, the supervisor rates employees on items running along a continuum from low to high, as from 1 to 5.

■ ■ ■ ■ ■ ■ ■

■ ■ ■ ■ ■ ■ ■ ■ ■ ■ ■

Employee Feedback Form

Is employee feedback built into your organization's evaluation form? If not, you may wish to check the feasibility of factoring a form like this into your appraisal process. Perhaps you can pilot it in your own department; then, if you're pleased with the results, suggest it be used organization-wide. The idea is to generate thinking from employees that will be helpful during the appraisal discussion, or as part of a mini-review. Just as importantly, it conveys the message that employee input counts. This form complements the "ice breaker" questions on pages 47 and 48.

Here are five questions that can help jump-start our appraisal discussion on [date]. Responding is voluntary, but I hope you'll think about responses and jot down your thoughts so we can discuss them during the appraisal discussion. The aim is to make sure we're both clear about how your work days can be as gratifying as possible. If you decide to answer, please bring this form to our discussion.

1. What work do you most enjoy doing? Are there a few areas that stand out?

2. What responsibilities most satisfied you during this review cycle?

3. Ideally, what would you like to do that you're not doing now?

_____

_____

_____

_____

_____

4. What would it take to do this? How can I help you?

_____

_____

_____

_____

_____

5. In what other ways can I help you?

_____

_____

_____

_____

_____

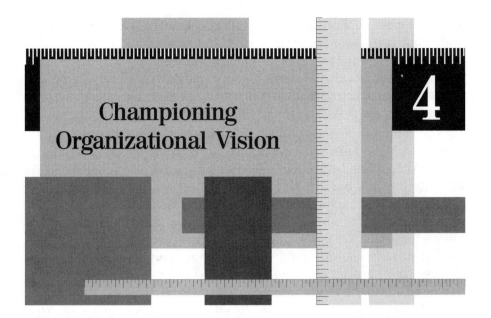

Championing Organizational Vision

4

T'is the good reader that makes the good book.
—Ralph Waldo Emerson, a boldly original
thinker, essayist, poet, and philosopher

Vision is sparked by passion, insight, even a goal that has wandered into unexpected territory. Sometimes it begins with a mistake. That's what happened in 1894, when 24-year-old Will Kellogg, brother of Battle Creek Sanitarium director, Dr. John Harvey Kellogg, was asked to run experiments on boiled wheat paste. Dr. Kellogg was hoping for more digestible bread for his patients. One batch, mistakenly left out overnight, dried out. Run through rollers and baked the next day, the paste turned into surprisingly tasty crispy flakes. The flakes were a hit with patients—and Will never turned back.[1] Vacationing with his family in 1951, Tennessee homebuilder Kemmons Wilson couldn't find consistently good accommodations on the road from Memphis to Washington, DC. Frustrated by shoddy motel quality, having to drive elsewhere for meals and, especially, by having to pay $2 apiece for each of his five children, Wilson vowed to bring change. He began planning Holiday Inns before he ever returned home. Societal shifts favored his plan, but Wilson's vision was simply "to bring standardization to the hotel industry so people would know exactly what to expect."[2] New groom Earle Dickinson was concerned that his bride kept cutting and burning herself while learning to cook. A cotton mill worker for surgical supplier Johnson & Johnson, he devised "bandages" that she could apply herself—small patches of gauze secured with adhesive tape. They worked so well that Dickinson took his concept to management. Band-Aids were introduced in 1921.[3]

These men drew many others to their vision. They had to, or their visions would have remained isolated. None of their products had a straight path to success. Band-Aid sales, in fact, stayed sluggish all through the 1920s, when they finally became single bandages rather than long strips that needed snipping. Dickinson was promoted to vice president.[4] All three men ran with their visions, individually at first, then through the organizations they built. Or in Dickinson's case, persuasively shaped. Each was mission-driven. As author W. Clement Stone understood, "When you discover your mission, you will feel its demand. It will fill you with enthusiasm and a burning desire to get to work on it."[5]

How do you ignite that mission on all levels of an organization? How do you keep the vision singing as it's translated into goals, objectives, and performance measures, tied up in budgets, and bounced about in often uncertain economies.

The motivation begins at the top. "Producing change is about 80 percent leadership—establishing direction, aligning, motivating and inspiring people—and about 20 percent management—planning, budgeting, organizing and problem-solving." But leadership, Harvard professor John Kotter also pointed out, "exists at all levels of an organization. At the edges of the enterprise, leaders are accountable for less territory. Their vision may sound more basic; the number of people to motivate may be two. But they perform the same leadership role as their senior counterparts. They excel at seeing things through fresh eyes."[6]

Top CEOs understand this. UPS's co-founder and former CEO, James Casey, is credited with not just pioneering a company, but building a culture. Yet he once admonished a reporter to "remember the story is to be about us—not about me. No single individual should be given a disproportionate share of the credit."[7] Louis V. Gerstner dedicated his book, *Who Says Elephants Can't Dance*, to "the thousands of IBMers who never gave up on the company, their colleagues, and themselves. They are the real heroes of the reinvention of IBM."[8] Southwest Airlines' Herb Kelleher said, " We hire great attitudes, and we'll teach them any functionality that they need."[9]

At a discussion in August 2001, Dr. Lionel Tiger, of Rutgers University, said, "Leaders often forget that people are predisposed to do a good job. I'm always impressed with the films in which the young player rushes up and says, 'Send me in, coach.' People are hardwired to want to be sent in. One of the things good leaders do is to allow people to do what is built into them to do anyway, which is to contribute."[10]

It's All About Values

But contribute how? Suppose an employee is working really hard, doing his or her best, yet still not doing what is best for the organization. This could mean the company's "core purpose" is not clear. "Core purpose reflects an organization's reason for being. An effective purpose reflects idealistic motivations for doing the company's work. It doesn't just describe an organization's output or target customers; it captures the soul of the organization."[11] For this soul to reach every cubicle, it needs to be genuinely integrated through all aspects of work. It can't just be a slogan on the wall, or even perk that says "good job," unless that job is designed to advance the organization's mission and the employee understands exactly what the perk represents. Trying to enlist employees in a "purpose" is futile if that purpose is not shining through in job descriptions, objectives, and performance measures. And supervisors and employees are bound to feel uncertain about their own value in an organization if the link from their work to organizational mission and values is not kept upfront.

Vision, strategy, and organizational structure really come down to values. Core values are the essential and enduring tenets of an organization. A small set of timeless guiding principles, core values require no external justification; they have *intrinsic* value and importance to those inside the organization. The Walt Disney Company's core values of imagination and wholesomeness stem not from market requirements but from the founder's inner belief that these qualities should be nurtured for their own sake. William Procter and James Gamble didn't instill in P&G's culture a focus on product excellence merely as a strategy for success but almost as a religious tenet. Service to the customer is a way of life at Nordstrom's that traces its roots back to 1901, eight decades before customer service programs became stylish. As Ralph S. Larsen, former Johnson & Johnson CEO, put it, "The core values embodied in our credo might be a competitive advantage. But that's not *why* we have them. We have them because they define for us what we stand for."[12]

Such convictions are the spirited force that Peter Drucker described as, "turning out energy larger than the sum of the efforts put in."[13]

Even with organizational principles firmly embedded, awareness of them might stay in the boardroom. Most employees may not even know they exist. For this reason, communicating an organization's vision and strategy to every employee should be viewed as an internal marketing campaign. The goals of such a campaign are identical to those of traditional marketing campaigns: to create awareness and to affect behavior.[14] Capturing the essence of core values and purpose is not an exercise in wordsmithery. The point is not to create a perfect statement but to gain a deep understanding of your organization's core values and purpose, which can then be expressed in a multitude of ways. In fact, it's suggested that once the core has been identified, managers [and their staff] can generate their own statements to share with the group.[15] The idea is not to spout a slogan but to get upfront and personal with an organization's raison d'etre, to mainstream its principles, and practice its values as a given of daily worklife.

■■■■■■■■■■■■

What's Personality Got to Do With It?[16]

Charles Farkas and Suzy Wetlaufer looked at how executives lead by analyzing interviews with 160 CEOs around the world. Five distinct approaches emerged. Al Zeien, former CEO of Gillette, for example, uses a classic "human assets" approach, personally conducting 800 performance reviews annually.

Strategy Approach

Believing their main job is to create, test, and design long-term strategies, these CEOs value people who can carry daily operations and have fine-tuned analytical skills.

Human-assets Approach

Formulating strategy close to home, these CEOs work to impart organizational values. They closely manage individual development, seek a satellite CEO group, and value long-term employees who demonstrate the "company way." Mavericks are not popular.

Expertise Approach

Because their key aim is to bolster competitive advantage, these CEOs tend to value employees willing to become immersed in a complementary expertise.

Box Approach

Dedicated to ensuring predictable experiences for customers and employees, these CEOs work to add value by creating, communicating, and monitoring specific financial and/or cultural controls. Because seniority counts, look for promotions from within.

Change Approach

These CEOs focus not on a specific point of arrival but on the process of getting there. As dedicated change agents, they seek passion, energy, and an openness to a reinvented tomorrow.

■ ■ ■ ■ ■ ■ ■

A worker without a clear purpose can become a directed producer if there's a sound link with organizational mission and strong recognition for contributing to it. This can become even more crucial in a down economy. Mary Hayes wrote in *InformationWeek* that "in tough times, companies are seeing the value of making sure employee goals are closely aligned with the goals of the business overall."[17] Once carefully tailored to mission and values, computer software can provide important support to this effort. Goal-alignment software lets business help employees develop goals, then issue reviews, bonuses, and merit pay according to their successful achievement. But does software that collects, categorizes, distributes, calculates and holds employees responsible for their career goals sound a bit like Big Brother? Faye Katt, vice president of global employee services and corporate counselor at Baxter Healthcare Corp, asks, "Are you empowering your employees, trusting them, and asking them to be responsive and results-oriented? Those are shared values, [and] such a system doesn't become Orwellian. It's about results, and if you're treating people fairly, it works." According to analyst Maria Schafer, communication is key. If you say, "We're going to be tracking you and watching you, who wants that?" Instead, she says that companies must show employees that they're stakeholders in their businesses and that the more insight they have into corporate strategies, the greater chance there is for their companies' success.[18]

NationsBank, now integrated with Bank of America, has put goal-alignment software in place with great success. Its software gathers relevant information from every organizational level and transmits it to executives as brief electronic reports. If executives want more detail about a given measure, they can double-click the item in the electronic report.

"As a result, managers at every level can readily see if targeted objectives are being met, can tell where the best performance is coming from, and reward those responsible."[19]

■ ■ ■ ■ ■ ■ ■ ■ ■ ■ ■ ■

Georgia-Pacific's Cascading Effect

"Georgia-Pacific recognized that its processes for reviewing and managing performance were cumbersome and, more important, did not always provide a clear link between employee activities and the goals of the organization. To restructure its performance management systems, the company designed a database, accessible to salaried management online and in real-time, that defines a standard competency set applicable to all employees. The Georgia-Pacific strategic planning process generates company goals and measures that are set in January and then cascaded to all levels of the organization. The new performance management process then links these organizational objectives to individual performance targets, establishing a clear link between objectives and daily employee activities."[20]

■ ■ ■ ■ ■ ■ ■

Doing Your Best vs. Doing What's Best for Your Company

A vision provides the focal point. Then, to manage performance effectively, employee performance is aligned with organizational goals. But as Peter Drucker wrote, "The real difficulty lies not in determining what objectives we need, but in deciding how to set them."[21] "How can both managers' and their boss' eyes be focused on what the job—rather than the boss—demands?"[22]

Communication is a vital start. "It's a two-way affair, and the receiver's function is no less important than that of the sender."[23] Regardless of whether there is buy-in, everyone at an organization can be expected to understand where his or her organization stands. And buy-in tends to grow as employees feel connected to a mission, understand why and how their contributions are significant, and have performance measures directly linking their specific contributions to organizational goals. Everyone also needs to be on board. As a cornerstone of strategic performance management, the performance appraisal needs to be recognized not as a perfunctory pain but as the valuable management tool it can become. As a mainstreamed asset, it can help drive the entire organization toward a shared vision that reflects proudly on everyone in the entire organization. "A team isn't really a team if it isn't going anywhere. And if the values, mission, goals and practices of a team don't match up, you're going to have a tough time as a team player."[24] Supervisors and other managers might, in fact, be appraised on how well their departments contribute to accomplishing strategic goals. For everyone to be on board, there needs to be a cascading effect, with accountability from the top. One Human Resources consultant, called in to train 180 supervisors on applying strategic goals to individual departments, learned quickly that the supervisors had no idea what these new goals were. They had not been shared—on any level—prior to the training.

Even supervisors grounded in goals usually can't just run with them. Training is helpful not just in implementing but also in helping to identify and frame goals. If "improve customer service by 30 percent" is a priority, every department in the organization should spell out what, how, over what time frame, and at what cost this will be addressed. No department should be left out. Each department can contribute, even if support for the front lines is indirect. The point is that everyone swims together.

Goal-directed performance appraisals might be viewed as a six-step process:

1. Establish business objectives and strategic goals.

2. Effectively communicate business objectives and goals.

3. Assess structure alignment with business objectives and goals.

4. Assess the employee's capacity to achieve business objectives and goals.

5. Fill in the gaps between capacity and business objectives and goals.

6. Implement, measure, and modify.[25]

When properly executed, an appraisal instrument can become a powerful tool for establishing corporate culture and ensuring that employees understand and act on the organization's broad strategic goals. In valuing diversity, for example, an organization might evaluate supervisory personnel in such areas as the following:[26]

▣ Implement diversity recruitment strategies to ensure that a diverse pool of applicants are identified for all vacant positions.

▣ Build time into regular staff meetings to discuss diversity issues.

▣ Communicate to employees that the organization does not tolerate racial, sexual, or other offensive jokes or storytelling, and that such behavior will lead to disciplinary action.

▣ Require all new employees to attend diversity training within six months of their hire date.

▣ Conduct business with vendors, consultants, and business partners that reflect a commitment to inclusion and diversity.

▣ Integrate diversity principles in key trainings.

■ ■ ■ ■ ■ ■ ■ ■ ■ ■ ■ ■ ■

Strategic Human Resources

Top management might begin to look toward the Human Resources Department as less of a "service only" department and more of a strategic unit, such as marketing. Why not invite the head of Human Resources and possibly other HR staff members to participate in the strategic planning process? Turn to him or her for ideas on how to use the performance appraisal process as a tool for attaining organizational goals. Don't stop at goal-setting. Craft a full plan that periodically measures effectiveness, rewards advances, and derails failure. Champion organizational vision as the framework in which all employees are expected to measure up, knowing they can count on informed, enthusiastic support along the way. Discussing vision's role in running an organization, Merck & Company Chairman and CEO Raymond Gilmartin said, "Everything you do is for a reason, and that reason is contained within the vision."[27] While there may be lots of interesting, creative byways, all employees should be able to find the main highway.

■ ■ ■ ■ ■ ■ ■

At Xerox, a "Performance Excellence Plan" translates corporate strategies into specific individual or team objectives and goals. Supervisors and employees come up with plans for the coming year, including clarity about how progress will be measured. Clearly spelled out is what the organization will expect. In Washington, DC, National Cooperative Bank has implemented a three-step approach. Management links company goals to team and individual performance goals, then all employees work with their supervisors to develop the next year's performance plan. The plan sets goals, establishes a mechanism for tracking progress, adjusts goals, and provides for "coaching" throughout the year as needed. Measurement criteria are built into the process. Then, management takes the process much farther—taking a broad view, a plan is generated to bolster the skills of all employees over the coming year, whether through coaching, training, and/or other kinds of professional education.

At the American Society for Training and Development, every employee has a calendar-based performance plan developed by both the employee and his or her manager. Together, they set up to six goals with at least three of them tied to metrics aligned with the organization's overall goals. The remainder tie specifically to the department and/or the individual. There is a formal six-month (mid-year) review where the employee and manager review progress to date. There may be other informal reviews based on the employee's project timelines and goals may be revised as necessary. At the end of the year, the employee conducts a self-assessment and the manager conducts a formal performance review. The manager and employee then discuss both reviews. Compensation is tied to this process, but is addressed separately.

The United States Army has a true cascade. Within the first 30 days of the rating period, warrant and commissioned officers sit down with their supervisors and develop major performance objectives. They review duty descriptions, knowledge required to perform these duties, and supervisory controls. Results must be aligned with those of their supervisors, whose objectives are aligned with those of their superiors. Each quarter, supervisors perform interim reviews with employees to discuss progress toward their objectives and revise them as needed. When the rating period ends, officers submit a summary of their accomplishments and are rated on a four-point scale.

Management by Objectives

Shifting the focus from past performance and ratings, Management by Objectives (MBO) encourages a supervisor/subordinate partnership approach that looks ahead. The focus is on goals to be achieved rather than merely looking back. Actively engaged in the process, the staff person has responsibility for managing his or her own job performance rather than just getting "marked" on what has already occurred.

Popular in private and public organizations,[28] the original MBO concept came from the accounting firm of Booz, Allen, and Hamilton, and was called a "manager's letter." The process consisted of having all the subordinate managers write a letter to their superiors detailing what their performance goals were for the coming year and how they planned to achieve them. The idea caught on at General Electric in the 1950s, and Douglas McGregor has since developed it into a philosophy of management.[29]

Beyond an evaluation program or process, MBO reflects an "entire philosophy of management practice, a method by which managers and subordinates plan, organize, control, communicate, and debate. By setting objectives through participation, or by assignments from a superior, the subordinate is provided with a course to follow and a target to shoot for while performing the job."[30] Goals are objective, often quantifiable, and just about always written.

Because this approach targets specific goals, it is critical that these goals be aligned with organizational vision and priority needs, not only across a company but within the department. Given their prominence, these are the goals that a staff person will feel most responsible for achieving.

Establishing MBO works like this:

◙ Employee creates a not-too-long goal list or employee and supervisor develop it together—goals are concrete, realistic and challenging and include time lines.

◙ Goals are considered in context of organizational mission and needs and department needs, along with talents and interests of the employee, including possible training or other support required to address goals.

◙ Goals may be modified as needed, then a written list of specific goals is mutually agreed to.

◙ A clear action plan is developed.

◙ Throughout the evaluation cycle, the supervisor informally encourages goal attainment and the employee takes the initiative to check in.

◙ At the end of the evaluation cycle, they meet to talk about outcomes and repeat process for upcoming cycle, possibly retaining some goals that have not yet been fully achieved.

How IBM Focuses Energy

"Every business, if it is to succeed, must have a sense of direction and mission, so that no matter who you are and what you are doing, you know how you fit in and that what you are doing is important," wrote former IBM CEO Louis V. Gerstner.[31]

IBM has instituted "Personal Business Commitment," a system that aligns company objectives with the activities of individual employees. "PBC helps [IBM] understand every individual's unique contribution to achieving corporate objectives and rewards employees accordingly. Managers can clearly see what is expected of their staff, how to measure activities, and how to tie them to company objectives. This kind of empowerment and accountability motivates people not just to do their best but also to focus their energies on doing what is best for the company." [32]

At the beginning of the year, all IBM employees sign a personal business commitment that states what they will deliver to the company. Employees align their personal commitments with IBM's overall business plan as:

1. Commitment to *win*.

2. Commitment to *execute*.

3. Commitment to contribute to the *team*.

Objectives incorporating the development of specific skills are tied to both individual commitments and business unit plans. These plans and commitments form the baseline against which performance will be evaluated.

Balanced Scorecards

One of the most important tools in the arsenal of MBO techniques, the balanced scorecard translates an organization's mission and strategy into a comprehensive set of performance measures. It looks at the big picture, building in measurable steps for strategic management. The aim is to foster a team approach to achieving organization-wide objectives.

"The Balanced Scorecard retains an emphasis on achieving financial objectives, but also includes the performance drivers of these objectives, [measuring] organizational performance across four balanced perspectives: financial, customers, internal business processes and learning and growth."[33]

Here's how it can work:

When a major corporation set the company-wide goal of improving customer service several years ago, it let none of its employees off the hook. Even those employees or departments who didn't interact with customers were encouraged to take part—by treating the in-house units to which they reported as customers. The chef in the cafeteria, for example, didn't meet with actual customers but began to regard the employees who ate in his cafeteria as his customers. The corporation's entire corporate culture is now infused with the commitment to recognize customer service. Visitors to its headquarters are often surprised and delighted to see messages about customer service emblazoned on the floors and engraved on doorways throughout the building.

You might institute a balanced scorecard approach in your organization by asking each employee to develop his or her own individual scorecard. Challenge the employee to come up with ways of supporting your organization across the four main areas, by assisting your organization to save dollars, attract and retain customers, improve internal business procedures, and contribute to your own and your colleagues' learning and growth.[34] The more involved an employee is in setting these parameters, the more enthusiastic they will be about achieving them.

Making Scorecards Work[35]

In 1996, accounting giant KPMG engaged in a study of seven European companies that had implemented scorecards. Only 30 percent had achieved their original stated goals, however, the majority of them were satisfied with the results. KPMG concluded that a balanced scorecard is an expensive way to raise awareness. As a result, it designed "The Ten Commandments of Scorecard Implementation."

Do:

- ☑ Know what you hope to achieve.

- ☑ Use the scorecard for implementation of strategic goals.

- ☑ Ensure goals are in place before the scorecard is implemented.

- ☑ Ensure that at least one top-level nonfinancial sponsor and line managers back the project.

☑ Implement a pilot before introduction.

☑ Carry out a pilot for each business unit before implementation for customization.

Don't:

☒ Use the scorecard for top-down control.

☒ Standardize the project with ready-made scorecards.

☒ Ignore training and communication.

☒ Overcomplicate the process or strive for perfection.

☒ Underestimate the extra administrative workload and cost.

☒ Leave the process to accountants or without top-down support.

Three Scenarios

Below links the performance appraisals of Marilyn, Richard, and Peg to the goals of their organizations:

Marilyn's law firm has set a goal of 15 percent revenue growth over the next 12 months. To reach this goal, the firm will hire seven associates. Because Marilyn coordinates new hires in her role as office administrator, she and the managing partner identified nine new objectives during her recent performance appraisal. Several give Marilyn the chance to enjoy new challenges plus do some of the traveling that she has been eager to do.

▣ Participate in on-campus recruiting at five law schools.

▣ Select attorneys who will conduct on-site interviews.

▣ Make sure all travel and related arrangements are made.

▣ Circulate the resumes of those screened.

▣ Create interview schedules for students at the firm.

▣ Distribute and explain the interview assessment form.

▣ Collect completed assessment forms, tally them, and present the results to the Managing Partner.

- ▣ Ensure follow-up letters are sent to all those interviewed.

- ▣ Coordinate final hiring details as requested by managing partner.

In his role as duplicating supervisor, Richard understands that his company must produce cutting-edge products to meet customer needs and stay competitive. Therefore, he is expected to continually learn all he can and stay on top of new developments. Given the situation with his ill mother, he has lagged in new training over the past several months. Loss of a recent order made the lag even more apparent. To meet organizational revenue, he worked out the following objectives with his supervisor, each of which advance organizational goals yet are attainable despite Richard's need to spend time with his mother. Over the next four months, Richard will be appraised on four new objectives:

- ▣ Identify and participate in two to four short-term training courses, including some that may be available online or during work time rather than the usual evening or Saturday seminars.

- ▣ Identify four to seven potential new customers and work with supervisor to set up a two-hour training demonstrating their company's newest capabilities.

- ▣ Follow up by phone with participants and assess level of interest, submitting report to supervisor.

- ▣ Meet with supervisor in four months to discuss how well these objectives have been met.

Given her continuing poor performance record, Peg's supervisor sits down with her and asks how she thinks she can be more helpful at their advertising agency. The question has an upbeat tone. It also puts more responsibility on Peg, making her accountable for a workload that, in part, she helps to shape. If Peg really doesn't want to begin contributing at an acceptable level, that will also be clear. The discussion generates three suggestions that, along with already assigned tasks, will drive Peg's performance. A follow-up discussion is scheduled in three weeks to review just these new objectives, each of which is geared toward strengthening customer service, a goal designed to help generate new business. A discussion is scheduled in six weeks to review Peg's progress on all of her objectives.

▣ Respond positively to clients by greeting them by name and ensuring that their requests are met within one day, alerting a supervisor if that is not feasible.

▣ Attend the weekly staff meeting, select one project that is discussed, and suggest a way to contribute to it. Ensure that front desk is covered during the full hour-long meeting, coordinating with supervisor to secure commitment two days in advance.

▣ Offer to help out at next week's exhibit showcasing campaigns developed for agency's clients over past year, again coordinating with supervisor so that front desk will be covered.

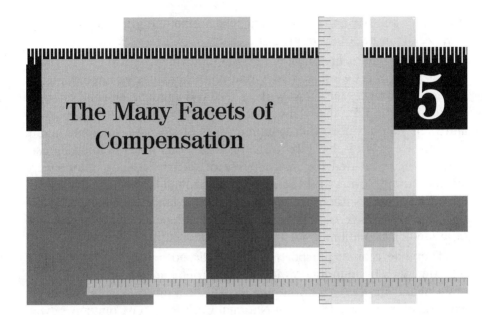

The Many Facets of Compensation

5

Not everything that can be counted counts, and not everything that counts can be counted.

—Albert Einstein, Nobel Prize winning physicist who revolutionized science.

Prior to the Industrial Revolution, it was not uncommon to think that the hungriest (literally) workers would be motivated to become the top performers and, therefore, should be kept at subsistence pay levels. Toward the end of the 18th century, the classical economics of Adam Smith took issue with this, holding that monetary incentives would motivate employees to work even harder.[1] A century later, Frederick W. Taylor, the "father of scientific management," sought the "one best way" and the one fastest way to get a job done.[2] An engineer at Midvale Steel Works in Philadelphia, Taylor used stopwatches to guide workers in most efficiently performing each of their tasks. With pay linked to productivity, workers who met production standards received 125 percent of their base pay. Workers who missed the standards received just 80 percent.

Pay for performance was a hot issue then. It still is today. But it's now clear that sustained productivity does not come out of a stopwatch. One study after another underscores that recognition and gratifying work, not pay, are the most potent motivators.

Pay, however, is inextricably tied to employment. Through the 1900s, America's workers witnessed an evolution in how they were paid. At the start of the 20th century, few workers received anything more than wages as compensation for their labor. With no modern-day benefits, workers and their families bore the economic risks of sickness, unemployment, and old age. "With charitable organizations sometimes helping, household savings provided the main source of security. Labor unions were adverse to employers and the government mingling in such worker affairs. This stance is traceable to the many in the labor movement that had an agrarian heritage of self-sufficiency and independence that provided little ideological rationale for bargaining for security benefits."[3]

There were other perspectives. The railroad industry led the way in the late 1800s by founding YMCAs along routes to minister to workers' physical and spiritual needs, hoping to provide a more reliable and stable workforce. In the late 1890s, the National Cash Register Company's "welfare division" experimented by building libraries, recreation facilities, and social clubs, and offering classes.[4] By 1920, John Wanamaker offered a medical clinic, a savings and loan, and life and pension insurance plans at his Philadelphia department store.[5] At Ford Motor and other companies welfare workers practiced "home visiting," extending a bit of warmth from an otherwise impersonal corporation.[6] But the sentiment of the time could be heard in the words of Samuel Gompers, president of the American Federation of Labor, who argued in 1917 that compulsory benefits "...weaken independence of spirit, delegate to outside authorities some of the powers and opportunities that rightfully belong to wage earners, and break down industrial freedom by exercising control over workers through a central bureaucracy."[7] "Labor's attitude toward self-sufficiency and independence would not weaken until some 15 years later under the devastation of the Great Depression."[8]

The latter part of the last century was characterized by changes in the structure of the economy and in American society that had started years earlier—a continuation of both the growth in importance of women in the workforce and the aging of the workforce, a change in the pattern of immigration, and a continuation of the shift towards the service sector. These changes led to an evolution in the way workers were compensated—aligning pay to organizational goals, tailoring compensation to employees' needs, and reconfiguring employee benefit plans.[9]

By the close of the 10th century, a typical worker received more than 25 percent compensation in the form of benefits.[10] And increasingly, creative incentives began filling up the workplace. On Fortune's list of "100 Best Companies to Work For," the semi-conductor maker Xilinix instituted a six-percent payout but a "no layoff" policy. J.M. Smuckers offers lots of paid time off to volunteer and lets employees be taste testers. Pella offers a $100 savings bond or a day off for perfect attendance. Adobe Systems has Friday night beer bashes, job rotations, and three-week paid sabbaticals every five years. MBNA provides a $20,000 adoption reimbursement and gives you $500 plus a limo and an extra vacation week when you get married. The Container Store, already offering one of retail's highest pay scales, has domestic partner benefits, free yoga classes, and even chair massages at headquarters.

But do all these perks really make a difference? Or are they actually disincentives? And are organizations generally paying for efforts or results? If results, are they short-term, or tied to genuine organizational goals? Early in the 21st century, we're still grappling with these basic compensation questions. The challenge is no longer whether to reward, but what to reward and how much. As part of performance management, a solid appraisal process can be an indispensable asset in sorting all this out.

■ ■ ■ ■ ■ ■ ■ ■ ■ ■ ■ ■ ■

How Does Your Employer Measure Up?

- ▣ How are pay decisions made?
- ▣ What gets rewarded here?
- ▣ How much does the organization value my position?
- ▣ How are different positions here valued?
- ▣ What are the pay ranges for my position?
- ▣ When was the last time our salary ranges were reviewed?
- ▣ Does our organization meet or lead market rates, or do we lag?
- ▣ Is there bonus money?
- ▣ Is there internal and external equity?
- ▣ What performance is expected for the compensation I receive?

■ ■ ■ ■ ■ ■ ■ ■

■ ■ ■ ■ ■ ■ ■ ■ ■ ■ ■ ■

Communicating About Pay: Shadowing the Appraisal

The discussion about pay is usually more effective when held apart from the performance evaluation. If not kept apart, talk about compensation can be distracting. Mentioned upfront, an employee may be mentally computing the new amount, or feeling down because it's less than anticipated. If kept to the end, the employee may wait tensely for the figure and fail to actively engage in the appraisal discussion. Either way, talk about pay might affect the entire discussion.

Pay, however, does shadow most formal evaluations. Employees will be eager to find out about future paychecks, and supervisors will either want to recognize good work with a tangible reward or perhaps just get past disappointing news (although there is ample feedback that shows delaying the discussion might be more likely). Pay is inextricably tied to appraisals, and it's fair for employees to expect that the compensation will be scheduled at the end of the appraisal meeting, or soon after.

At the meeting, the supervisor should be prepared to thoroughly explain *why* and *how* the salary decision was made, not just in the context of the employee's performance but in line with overall compensation decisions. If an employee would have received more in better economic times, he or she has the right to know it. If there is a tight pool and others have performed more effectively, that should be communicated honestly as well. The supervisor needs to clarify what the raise is based on, the range of possible increase amounts, and the reasoning that supports the sum awarded.

If supervisors have stayed on top of appraisals through a series of mini-discussions, and employees have stayed actively engaged, the discussion about money should include no real surprises. If there are surprises, supervisors might question whether they said anything misleading, and employees might question whether there are real lags in their performance and, if so, what it will take to correct them.

■ ■ ■ ■ ■ ■ ■

What Is Compensation?

Defined in its broadest sense, compensation is any reward or payment given to a person for services performed. Operationally, that definition tends to narrow according to the definer's perspective. Managers typically define compensation as the financial rewards package provided to employees in exchange for their services—wages, salaries, commissions and bonuses, plus insurance and other types of indirect monetary benefits. Employees generally define compensation more narrowly, as the wage or salary received from employers for work performed.[11]

The difference is not subtle. With perhaps 25 percent or more of compensation existing in benefits, most employees are receiving significantly more than the bottom-line net check they take home each week. It's not unusual for employees to be happily surprised when their benefits are quantified—not just as numbers in paychecks that may not be scrutinized regularly but as a concrete breakdown that is flagged during the compensation discussion phase of the performance appraisal.

"The *total* rewards package has three purposes:

1. To **attract** a sufficient number of qualified workers to fill organizational positions.

2. To **retain** employees so that turnover is held to acceptable levels.

3. To **motivate** employees to perform to the fullest extent of their capabilities."[12]

Organizational rewards packages are usually structured with three main components:[13]

1. **Direct Monetary Rewards**. Sometimes called cash compensation, direct rewards include everything (for example, salary, wage, commission) that an employee is paid for work accomplished or effort expended. This income is discretionary.

2. **Indirect Monetary Payments**. Usually called benefits, these payments include items of financial value that do not result directly in employees' receiving spendable dollars. They cover various forms of protection, such as health, life and disability insurance, and services, such as uniforms, free parking, financial counseling, and employer subsidized cafeterias.

3. **Psychological Satisfactions**. Psychic income is key in work environments. This compensation includes recognition, opportunities to perform meaningful work, social interaction, job training, advancement possibilities and a host of similar factors.

Two fundamental compensation philosophies tend to drive thinking:

The **entitlement philosophy** is often characterized by cost-of-living raises and across-the-board pay increases. Eligibility is longevity-based. There is either a general pay increase for all employees, the same increase for all employees within a classification, or a step increase within a pay grade or range.[14] While the performance appraisal is crucial for feedback, development and other purposes, it provides little, if any, assistance when pay is entitlement-based.

The **performance-based philosophy** entails a variable pay approach in which pay goes up or down based on a measure of performance. Not everyone in the same job will be paid exactly the same, and not everyone will like the approach.[15] By documenting performance that can support or douse a pay increase, performance appraisals are usually a vital aspect of performance-based compensation.

Then there's IBM. When Lou Gerstner took the helm in 1993, IBM was on its way to losing $16 billion and on the endangered species list. Gerstner shook everything up, transforming IBM culturally and competitively. In 1994, he brought sweeping compensation change, all designed "to bring the compensation system in line with the new IBM. I wanted to underscore my belief that you can't transform institutions if the incentive programs are not aligned with your new strategy."[16] In his candid book, *Who Says Elephants Can't Dance?*, Gerstner detailed how he realigned IBM's incentives to drive a new culture of teamwork and accountability dedicated to IBM's bottom-line success (and survival).

Bonuses were paid to executives based solely on the performance of their individual units. If your operation did well but the overall corporation did poorly, it didn't matter. You still got a good bonus...Beginning in 1994, we instituted a huge change. All executives would have some portion of their annual bonus determined by IBM's overall performance...except for those people who reported directly to me. Their bonuses were to be based entirely on the company's over-all performance. Executives at the next level were paid 60 percent based on overall performance and 40 percent on their business unit results…the system cascaded from there. Of all the changes I made in 1993 and 1994, nothing else had the impact of this move in sending a message that, 'We need to work together as a team. Gerstner's not kidding. He really wants us to make integration the centerpiece of our new strategy'…In the mid-1990s, we introduced variable pay globally across IBM. This was our way of saying to all IBMers that if the company could pull off its turn-around, each and every one of them would share in the rewards. Over the next six years, $9.7 billion was paid out to IBMers world-wide.[17]

■ ■ ■ ■ ■ ■ ■ ■ ■ ■ ■ ■

Talking About Dollars

The best of supervisor/employee relationships can get sticky when it comes to compensation. This is especially true when a tight financial pool must be distributed among several highly deserving team members. Here's a look at how Mark (employee) and Carol (supervisor) candidly address his justifiable request for a financial reward and her justifiable need to dole out limited dollars fairly. Both hold their ground, yet engage in a respectful give-and-take as Mark's performance appraisal comes to a close:

Carol: *Mark, I looked over the contributions you made recently and I'm so pleased. The coordination you handled and the research you applied to our new series of public seminars are terrific. You really helped the department by designing and conducting that needs assessment. The new products were just what our customers wanted. You were critical to the launch of those products, too. And as a result of your outreach and creative client communications, this year's first five product seminars were filled to capacity. I don't know who worked harder on them than you.*

Mark: *Thanks for noticing all that. I spent a lot of time on those efforts and think my input really helped.*

Carol: *I'll make sure you get a copy of this appraisal. As you've just seen, your contributions are highlighted in the summary section. And I'll definitely be thinking about another opportunity for you to use your creativity and perseverance.*

[Carol stands up to close discussion]

Mark: *Gee, I'd like to discuss one more point with you. Didn't you just tell me I worked harder than anyone else? And that my efforts resulted in some real success for us, some additional revenue?*

Carol: *Yes. I also put that in writing on the appraisal form.*

Mark: *Well, this is a little awkward, but I feel I merit something more for all of the extra time I put in. I spent five complete weekends in a row working on this project, and also many late evenings. I brought in 25 new customers this quarter and worked on the committee to design an online customer order form. There have already been more than 1,000 hits on it.*

Carol: *We'll be talking about increases at another meeting, Mark. This one is just to assess your performance, which is excellent. But I do want you to know that I don't have a lot of flexibility with increase amounts. I have to spread a finite amount among all six of you on my team. I'm not at liberty to discuss your coworkers, but I value each of you for your unique strengths.*

Mark: *But you said I worked harder than anyone.*

Carol: *I recognized you for your efforts, but please understand that other members of the team have done a series of similar projects—most have also been successful and generated additional revenue. What I plan to do is distribute the increases in an equitable way. I do have access to a small discretionary fund that I use for one-time bonuses. I'm glad you pointed out those additional contributions. I plan to look at all the data and make those awards next week. I promise you'll know something soon.*

Mark: *I hope all of my work will count.*

Carol: *I won't forget you, Mark. Your work is excellent, and I appreciate it. But until I take a comprehensive look at our budget and a just distribution, I cannot commit to anything. Thank you for being patient.*

■ ■ ■ ■ ■ ■ ■

■ ■ ■ ■ ■ ■ ■ ■ ■ ■ ■ ■ ■

What Counts?

Employees aren't the only ones appraised by their companies. Jobs themselves undergo a process of evaluation and analysis, in part for the purpose of establishing a pay structure. "Job Evaluation" is the process of analyzing and ranking all the jobs in a given organization to determine the value of each job in relation to the others. Organizations generally use one of three methods:

◙ **Classification Method.** Pioneered by the federal government, this approach seeks to identify common skill sets, expertise, or responsibilities across a wide range of different job descriptions. A supervisor with an MBA who manages ten to 20 employees would be classified with a similar supervisor elsewhere in the organization, even if one were working in manufacturing and the other in marketing.

◙ **Ordering Method.** Sometimes called "The Ranking Method," this approach is much more subjective. A special committee, usually comprised of both management and employee representatives, hammers out the relative rank of each job in the company without making use of specific weighting criteria. The committee simply asks, "Which is more important to us—Job A or Job B?" This method works well for small organizations, but it can be very difficult to administrate in companies with hundreds of positions.

◙ **Point Method.** This is perhaps the most objective (but also the most complicated) of the three approaches. In this method, management assigns a point value to each of the skills, education levels, or other requirements necessary to do a given job. The job of nuclear engineer, for example, would be assigned many more education points than that of file clerk. Add up all the points and the organization has objective criteria for comparing jobs and establishing pay structures. It takes plenty of work to put a point system in place, but afterwards the organization has a fair, reliable, and objective system that can work for years.

■ ■ ■ ■ ■ ■ ■

It's Not Just About Pay

At IBM, compensation became quantifiable and clear. A group incentive for success was built in. But given the shaky structure, Gerstner inspired much more than profits. He cut through a demoralized bureaucracy and tapped into pride.

"Money is not the only incentive for people to stay with a company. In yet another survey, a 1998 "American @ Work" survey conducted by The Loyalty Institute of Aon Consulting in Chicago, 1,800 employees ranked pay only 11th as a reason for remaining with an employer, behind such factors as open communication with managers, ability to challenge the status quo, and opportunities for personal growth."[18]

Pay has substantive and symbolic components. In signaling what and who in the organization is valued, pay both reflects and determines the organization's culture. Therefore, managers must make sure the messages sent by pay practices are intended. Talking about teamwork and cooperation and then not having a group-based component to the pay system matters because paying solely on an individual basis signals what the organization believes is actually important—individual behavior and performance. Talking about the importance of all people in the organization and then paying some disproportionately more than others belies that message.[19]

Senior management at Quantum, the California disk drive manufacturer, demonstrates commitment to teamwork by placing every employee, from the CEO to hourly workers, on the same bonus plan, tracking everyone by the same measure—return on total capital. Men's Warehouse, the enormously successful off-price retailer, pays higher than the industry average, has fewer than 15 percent part-time staff, and funds extensive training. The issue isn't what their employees cost but what they can do—sell effectively because of knowledge and sales skills. Southwest Airlines, the industry leader in cost and productivity, succeeds with no individual incentives.[20] Southwest's compensation practices entail several simple elements: comparatively heavy use of collective, as contrasted with individual, awards such as profit sharing and stock ownership rather than individual pay for performance; relatively low executive pay; and consistent treatment—no giving executives big raises as employees are being asked to accept wage freezes and layoffs. Asked what motivated Southwest's performers to stay where the pay is below-market, the answer was "happiness."[21]

Performance appraisals send powerful messages about organizational values. The care with which they are developed, *if* they are developed, and how timely and tailored they are tell employees how much they are valued. And the extent to which employees participate in the process reflects their commitment as well. Given that appraisals themselves can be awkward and "pay is a difficult topic of conversation in most organizations...altogether taboo in many workplaces [and] simply not discussed unless absolutely necessary,"[22] the coupling of a genuine talk about evaluation and pay may be a conversation still waiting to happen. How pay is structured, and the thoroughness with which a manager addresses it, "reflect a fundamental [organizational] belief about people, motivation and management."[23]

It's an important conversation to have. Having an attractive benefits package is not enough. Employees must have ample knowledge of all benefits available and the value of those benefits. But research has indicated that the typical employee was able to recall less than 15 percent of the benefits received from the company. Effective communication is apparently the exception rather than the rule.[24] This is unfortunate because, beyond the "how much," employees care about understanding the "why" of their pay. "While the actual amount is very important, they want to know the rationale behind it. Research has shown that pay satisfaction increases with understanding of the pay scheme."[25]

Employees must see rewards as fair and equitable. Motivation will not flourish unless they do. Equity theory emphasizes that an individual is concerned not only with the absolute rewards for efforts contributed, but also, and perhaps more importantly, with the relationship of his or her rewards and efforts to the rewards and efforts of others.[26] Employees' comfort levels with compensation and recognition for work performed will also help shape other factors, such as turnover, absence, and attendance, all of which are directly linked to overall organizational morale, productivity, and competitiveness.

By developing a keen understanding of organizational compensation policy, and bridging that knowledge with specifics linked to individual employees, managers have an opportunity to build trust and strengthen communication in an area that is often difficult. Managers can be terrific ambassadors in showcasing company benefits and organizational values.

■ ■ ■ ■ ■ ■ ■ ■ ■ ■ ■ ■

Communicating About Pay[27]

Specificity Is Key

A manager's promise of a "good increase" may not look so good to an employee. A remark such as, "I'm going to get you the most I can," may build unrealistic expectations. "It is important to work out the details beforehand so that specifics can be clearly communicated...No chance of misunderstanding or false expectations can be permitted."

Pay Is Relative

"Each individual has a unique set of personal circumstances that make a given number high or low...same for the company." Supervisors should understand the "reference point," the factors such as performance, market, and economy that go into compensation, and explain them. Explaining can mean the difference between a disappointed, frustrated employee and a disappointed employee who sees the bigger picture and appreciates being told about it.

All Pay Is Not Created Equal

Base pay and bonuses, the most common forms of direct cash compensation, require different discussions. Talk about base pay is more general and balanced. Market practices, budget realities, and pay range are reference points. Bonuses offer a terrific motivational opportunity. "Handing money to an employee while discussing actions and behaviors [you] would like to see repeated creates a powerful link between performance and reward."

■ ■ ■ ■ ■ ■ ■

■ ■ ■ ■ ■ ■ ■ ■ ■ ■ ■ ■

People-based Pay[28]

The bureaucratic job-based approach used to determine pay won't be the major format driving pay system designs of the 21st century. Instead, the new designs will be people-based, driven by today's service and knowledge sectors.

Skill-based Pay

Master new skills and boost earnings. No one receives a raise or promotion until new proficiency is demonstrated. Instead of a job description, "person" and "skill block" descriptions are developed.

Direct observation, testing, and measurable results are among the evaluation tools. Polaroid Corporation has adopted this design. Proctor & Gamble has implemented it in 30 plants.

Knowledge-based Pay

Be rewarded for acquiring additional knowledge, either on the current job or a new one.

Credential-based Pay

Be recognized for having a license or diploma, or passing examinations given by a third party professional or regulatory agency.

Feedback Pay

Job descriptions become mission statements aligned with strategic business objectives that establish a direct link to an employee's role in accomplishing them.

Competency-based Pay

Subjective measures, not usually considered, are added to skills, knowledge, and credentials. Motives, values, self-image, and even social role might be included. Because of breadth, it's difficult to place a dollar value on this model.

■ ■ ■ ■ ■ ■ ■

Pay for Performance

Pay for performance is a sweeping term that describes a broad range of pay practices. While not meant as an entitlement, repeated annual increases not linked to specific performance achievement might be considered entitlements. Pay for performance is intended to link a worker's actions to the well-documented level of performance. Despite the necessary commitment of management time and administrative complexity, nearly one out of six organizations use such systems.[29]

Just as the appraisals they're often tied to, salary structures have changed over time. The traditional structure reflects a hierarchical approach, with minimum to maximum ranges and grades and narrow pay bands. There may be a few dozen such ranges. This structure often supports traditional **merit pay** programs driven by appraisal systems yielding overall numerical scores. Perceived as being more objective than other structures, the traditional structure is often an integral part of an organization's management style.[30]

Base pay, also a traditional form of compensation, provides direct compensation not affected by weekly productivity. However, the performance appraisal system and a job market study of average pay rates is crucial in justifying and determining an increase in base pay.[31]

Skill-based pay focuses on the fundamental knowledge, skills and abilities required of a position. But developing the performance criteria for assessing a skill can be very time consuming, and over time the skills may become outmoded, replaced by technological developments. And then what is to be done with the worker? Reduce his or her pay for the obsolete skills? Provide the worker more pay for achieving the replacement skills?[32]

Variable pay can work for individual, team, or organizational performance, perhaps as a bonus or some form of incentive payment. In executive compensation programs, stock options might be included. Variable pay generally requires a more fine-tuned performance appraisal system because it is outcome-oriented. For variable pay to generate worker interest and energy, the expectations must be realistic and the rewards for achieving these outcomes must be meaningful. Nevertheless, from a financial standpoint, variable pay can be a very appealing alternative to base pay increase systems. Variable pay does not compound from year to year. Funds not spent can be reused in the current year or the next budget cycle. "Having employees re-earn their performance bonus each year creates a compelling reason for them to improve instead of relaxing into an entitlement mentality, which is often the result of base pay increase programs."[33] Implementing a variable pay program is not without its problems. According to a study reported by the American Compensation Association in 1998, nearly 40 percent of variable pay plans had failed.[34]

Piece-rate pay is a form of variable pay where worker output (number of widgets produced) is easily measurable and directly linked to a worker's compensation. Pay can vary from day to day or hour to hour. Often, the worker receives a base rate. Added compensation is based on output above a predetermined standard. A mode of "Taylorizing" the workplace, a piece-rate system can be administered without any formalized performance appraisal system. **Gainsharing** aims to build productivity by sharing organizational gains from that productivity with those responsible. There may, for example, be rewards for saving time or dollars. While gainsharing outcomes are often quantifiable, they can vary considerably from one work unit to another, making consistency in performance appraisal difficult.

An alternate structure, the fast emerging use of **broadbands**, accommodates today's flatter organizational structure by eliminating narrowly defined jobs. Broadbanding emphasizes skills development and gives employees more freedom to move laterally or up and down within a pay grade. An employee desiring to downshift to a less stressful position, for instance, could do that without suffering a drastic pay cut. Broadbanding recognizes that 21st century employees often perform not one but several different jobs.[35]

Under broadbanding, pay decisions rest largely with managers—and the performance appraisal can be key. Entry-level employees with minimal qualifications begin at the first stop of their range. But rather than annual increases, advancement depends on performance. All raises become individually-determined merit raises. On the downside, managerial discretion opens possibilities of favoritism and abuse of the broadbanding structure.[36]

Incentives…or Disincentives?

More than 50 years ago, behavioral scientist Frederic Herzberg concluded that, "If you want people to do a good job, give them a good job to do."[37] Herzberg found that achievement and recognition are motivators. Pay becomes an issue only when it's inadequate, in which case it's a "dissatisfier." As reflected below, today's employers seem boundless in their quest to give recognition. There are rewards for every reason. But however creative, how well do all these perks work?

Alfie Kohn, a leading writer on money and motivation, questioned whether the rewards work for the long-term interest of the company, or for some short-term personal goal. Kohn indicated that noncash rewards don't engender increased quality, productivity, or creativity. He pointed out that "one of the most thoroughly replicated findings in social psychology is that the more you reward people, the more they tend to lose interest in whatever they did to get the reward. When interest declines, so does quality. 'You can get people to do more of something or faster for a little while if you provide an appealing reward. But no scientific study has ever found a long-term enhancement of the quality of work as a result of any reward system,'" Kohn said.[38]

CEO and president Bob Rodin eliminated individual incentives for the 1,800 employees at his electronic components firm. He analyzed the five-year earning potential of each, then assigned salaries. Regardless of salary, profit-sharing reflecting corporate performance was set at the same percentage for each employee. "Our company was divided by internal promotions and contests. We weren't working with a common vision," he said. "We eliminated these distractions." Productivity per employee almost tripled.[39]

"People seek, in a phrase, an enjoyable work environment."[40] Investigating successful companies characterized by motivated employees and low turnover despite competitive markets, Jeffrey Pfeffer found that "one of the core values at each company is fun." In *Six Dangerous Myths About Pay*, he described what employees value at the SAS Institute in North Carolina, the largest privately held company in the software industry:

Employees said they were motivated by SAS's unique perks—"plentiful opportunities to work with the latest and most up-to-date equipment and the ease with which they could move back and forth between being a manager and being an individual contributor. They also cited how much variety there was in the projects they worked on, how intelligent and nice the people they worked with were, and how much the organization cared for and appreciated them."[41]

Robert McNamara is quoted as saying that, "Brains like hearts go where they are appreciated." Southwest Airlines, one of the companies Jeffrey Pfeffer studied, drives this notion home. The point repeatedly underscored by organizational theorists is that when core values are conveyed by recognition on many levels, when incentives capture organizational principles and genuinely honor employee dedication and talent, they can work exceptionally well. When awards are just exercises in giving awards, and an organization's core values are not defined and embedded at all levels of the organization, awards will tend to fall flat after initial interest. To sustain employee motivation, there needs to be more than a symbolic pat on the back...unless the pat is truly earned and the act of giving it heartfelt.

How does Southwest motivate performance? "Through personal pride," a station manager said. He explained how the airline uses rewards to motivate performance:

"Customers send letters to headquarters, with compliments or complaints, about 5,000 per month. These letters are sent to the relevant station, then when I get it I will put a smiley fact sticker on it and frame it. People like to see their name up there. We have agent of the month awards in every department. The winners are chosen by their fellow employees...We also use $5 meal vouchers to reward people for good performance. Supervisors do this. And agents reward each other by sending Love Reports."[42]

At its core, Southwest has a team culture in which such initiatives can fly. When there are flight delays, for example, it's assumed that a situation rather than a person is at fault.

Recognition matters. In *1001 Ways To Reward Employees*, Bob Nelson offers a treasure chest of positive and creative reinforcements—everything from low-cost, no-cost, and fun awards, to attendance and safety awards, team awards, self-development awards, and sales goal awards. Research by Dr. Gerald Graham throughout the United States revealed that the type of reward employees most preferred was personalized spur-of-the-moment recognition from their direct supervisors. And a survey of American workers found that, in fact, 63 percent ranked a pat on the back as a meaningful incentive.[43]

In addition to other opportunities, ensuring a series of informal evaluations throughout the year, rather than just the yearly appraisal "event," builds in the time to provide recognition that employees and supervisors value. It's instructive that, according to one study, just 41 percent of surveyed employees believe that the average company listens to employees' ideas. The average American worker makes only one or two suggestions per year. The average Japanese worker submits hundreds of suggestions to his or her employer annually.[44]

■■■■■■■■■■■■

Ingenuity at Work

Recommending that awards be matched to the person and achievement, and be timely and given in context, Bob Nelson offers a mosaic of positive reinforcement in *1001 Ways To Reward Employees*.[44] To keep rewards fresh and valued, he suggests pacing them: for every four informal awards, such as a "thank you," provide a more formal acknowledgment, such as a day off; for every four of these present an even more formal reward, such as a plaque or well-developed praise at a company meeting; and ultimately, offer a raise, promotion, or special assignment. Nelson includes these adaptable ideas:

▣ Employees at Apple Computer, who worked on the first Macintosh, had their signatures placed inside of their product.

- The City of Philadelphia ran an electronic message around a downtown skyscraper citing the school system head.

- Eastman Kodak has a Humor Task Force.

- Reader's Digest provides space for employee gardens.

- Time Warner employees moved to new corridors and had a block party.

- Each year several Shell Oil employees trade positions with their United Kingdom counterparts.

- Retirees at H. B. Fuller in St. Paul have first crack at part-time jobs.

- Meeting certain sales levels at State Farm means dollars for Special Olympics.

Pay Online

Employees and supervisors can access compensation information anytime. But search carefully. Most frequently you'll get broad salary ranges. Compensation philosophies are rarely spelled out. Sometimes just a portion of the market is surveyed. There may be a charge. Unless there is detail about job descriptions, you may be looking at a level or job that is not what you want.

www.careerbabe.com/salarysites.html

www.careers.wsj.com/

www.jobstar.org/tools/salary/index.htm

www.salary.com

www.wageweb.com

www.salaryexpert.com

www.salarypower.com

www.ecomponline.com

www.bls.gov

With several New England locations, Stew Leonard's Dairy is on Fortune's "100 Best To Work For" list. Believing in both instant recognition and that "what gets rewarded gets repeated," the company recognizes employees with "Moo Notes." In 2002, supervisors gave out more than 20,000 such notes. A free lunch comes with the note, and a copy is placed in the employee's personnel file.

Three Scenarios

Applying compensation considerations to the three people who show up throughout this book, Marilyn warrants extra incentives, Richard requires candor and support and, based on her continuing poor performance, Peg merits no increase.

Because Marilyn is such a consistently good performer, but already at the top of her range, she is slated for a substantial bonus. Her firm wants to keep her. As an added demonstration of appreciation, Marilyn might also receive a significant nonfinancial benefit. A thoughtful and very special perk might be free parking or attendance at her law firm's retreat.

Richard's history of solid performance serves him well during this difficult period when his mother is so ill. But work concerns need to be discussed openly. If Richard's work continues to slip, his next rate increase will be affected. For the time being, it's not. Richard also receives other support, including the opportunity to explore telecommuting, a compressed work week, or time-off under the Family and Medical Leave Act.

Peg's poor performance still shows no improvement. Giving her any type of financial or nonfinancial recognition will be sending the wrong message. Acknowledging the problems, and documenting them as they occur, doesn't appear to be making a difference. Peg's last chance is a Performance Improvement Plan (Chpater 8), which she agrees to try.

Beware of Rating Errors

6

I don't know that there are any shortcuts to doing a good job.

—Sandra Day O'Connor, first female appointed
to the U.S. Supreme Court (1981)

When employees trust their supervisors to conduct fair and unbiased appraisals, their satisfaction with the system increases dramatically.[1] Intrinsic to this satisfaction is that the process stays trustworthy. If the process breaks down toward the end because of rating errors, the whole effort is tainted. Awareness of what these errors are, and how they affect performance evaluations, is critical to both employees and their supervisors. Employees need to stay vigilant, and the good intent of managers must be accompanied by the skill, understanding, and training required to downsize rating errors as much as humanly possible.

Even then it's difficult. While software is now marketed to support some types of evaluations, performance appraisals are a human process— conceived, developed, and administered by human beings. No performance evaluation comes with a flaw-free guarantee. Peter Drucker is clear that performance cannot be fully measured. "As each human being is unique, we cannot simply add them together, or subtract them from one another. ...to arrive at meaningful measurements is one of the greatest challenges to management."[2]

While goal-based systems are often seen as the best current option for rating performance, care must be taken when these systems are used. The kinds of behaviors that are specified in the goal-setting process are exactly what the employee will tend to focus on. It is therefore critical that these are the behaviors the organization wants to encourage.[3] Examples can be drawn from the composites introduced in Chapter 2. Because Marilyn takes great pride in being cited for outstanding interpersonal relationships, there is some danger that she may not insist that some work move as fast as required. Richard's goal of processing a high number of duplicating orders per week may undercut quality and, in fact, hurt business. While Peg's poor performance must be addressed at every level, it may be that a responsibility such as helping with typing overloads is being underscored at the expense of paying attention to effective phone protocols. This is another instance in which customer service may suffer.

Rater Bias

Focus on the dynamics of worker characteristics appears to have surfaced close to a century ago. Workplace awareness of individual needs and differences goes back to at least the early 20th century. In England, the work of Charles Darwin popularized ideas that individuals differed from each other in ways that were important. In France, the work of Alfred Binet and Theophile Simon led to the development of the first intelligence tests, and during World War I several armies tried using these tests to better assign soldiers to jobs. By 1923, *Personnel Management* was spelling out how to match a person's skills and aptitudes with job requirements.[4]

Performance evaluations rose on the wave of other personnel practices designed, in part, to reduce the potential for labor unrest. Companies began introducing formal job analysis to aid in employee selection and rationalize the hodgepodge of wage rates that existed in many companies.[5] In numerous formats, performance evaluations have been evolving ever since.

Bias in the process is well documented. A 15-year study released in 2002 by Pennsylvania State University reveals a pattern of employment practices that has historically helped men get promoted to upper-management positions. The study showed that employers make decisions based on "impression management," which is the ability of employees to shape and manage a self-image that positively influences others. Women were shown to be "low self-monitors," less concerned with crafting an impressionable image than men, who proved to have a "chameleon-like quality" enabling them to adapt skillfully to changing social climates. "When employee promotions are based on subjective evaluations rather than skills and talent, men have the edge, with a 15 percent higher chance of being promoted."[6] Another study at a midwestern university found that students rated the same person differently when viewing her on video during pregnancy, and then five months later. When asked about such characteristics as "dependability" and "ability to do the job," the students "with a remarkably high degree of consistency," assigned her a lower rating during pregnancy, despite the fact that her behavior in both tapes was the same.[7]

Evaluation problems also emerge because of perceptual differences in definitions. When words such as poor, fair, adequate, satisfactory, and excellent are used, the evaluation can be distorted. Exactly what does each mean? In comparison with whom? Is every employee being rated by the same standard?

Performance appraisals can get caught in a web of rating errors. Following are some of the most common:

Common Rating Errors

Halo Effect

This error occurs when an outstanding quality becomes the basis of an entire rating. Every performance dimension benefits as a result. But the halo effect represents an error only when the rating is not justified. There is a difference between halo errors and a true halo, which is justified by across-the-board excellent performance. Some organizations ask raters to evaluate everyone on a single dimension before proceeding to the next. The aim is to encourage raters to focus on a particular dimension rather than overall performance. Another method frequently used is "reverse wording," which structures forms so that a favorable answer for the first question might be ten on a scale of one to ten, while a favorable response to the sixth question might be one on the same scale. Again, the evaluator is required to focus on each question separately. The halo effect is sometimes attributed to favorable first impressions that stay intact despite evolving problems.

Horns Effect

This error is the reverse of the halo effect. Rather than one positive feature being projected onto all rating dimensions, a negative impression takes hold. An overall poor rating emerges because a negative performance in one area brings down all the others. If a sales manager, for example, receives a poor rating for turning in paperwork late, that rating might be extended to sales skills that are excellent. Careful documentation of sales closings through the year would be one effective way of addressing that kind of unjustified evaluation.

Sunflower Effect

Managers may become nervous that just rating employees as "average" will reflect poorly on them. As a result, all employees receive top ratings. But the opposite can be true. Supervisors' supervisors may question the ratings and conclude that inadequate time was devoted to conducting a careful review. During an exit interview at one major association, the departing employee, when asked his perspective on performance appraisals, responded that they were a joke. This despite the fact that his ratings were among the highest in the entire association. "Don't get me wrong," he said. "I like the increases, but I'm not doing my best work. I want to learn more and either my supervisor doesn't care about understanding the work of different employees, or she just doesn't care."

Leniency or Harshness Error

One rater may tend to be lenient or tougher with employees; several raters may all have different value systems. When appraisals apply words like "adequate" and "good," standards might not be defined clearly enough to ensure consistency throughout an organization. Some raters just tend to mark high; others low. It's often why employees report feeling as if they're back in school—and frustrated. Two employees producing similar results may receive quite different ratings from their respective supervisors simply because of these supervisors' tendencies to rate high or low. This error is also called positive or negative leniency. Evaluators report that "it motivates employees and makes them feel good."[8] Negative leniency may be justified as "nobody's perfect." The tendency is particularly strong when raters are rushed.[9] Rankers may be asked to check their evaluations to find out whether there's a pattern toward leniency or harshness. As one remedy, raters are asked to distribute their ratings, with percentages designated for the number of employees rated as excellent, good, adequate, and poor. This remedy is contrived and can unjustly place employees in false categories simply to respond to percentage demands.

Central Tendency Error

Some raters are reluctant to stretch high or low. They rate all employees as average and fail to distinguish between the star performers and those who need specific support. Also called the clustered ratings error and scale shrinking, this method takes away the need to make judgments. It's sometimes used by raters who feel they don't know an employee well enough to come up with an actual rating. By sticking to the middle, these evaluations are less useful when it comes to making personnel decisions, such as promotions, salary increases, training, counseling, and even feedback. Raters who demonstrate central tendency error can be shown the bigger picture so they understand how their ratings are distorting the evaluation process. Sometimes organizations ask that employees be ranked so they don't all end up in the middle. But imposing a bell curve disbursement of employees' ratings can create other problems. Forcing the hand of a manager in an effort to arrive at predetermined ratings, or at a distribution that supports the increased budget, is not fair to employees and can lead to serious morale and legal problems.

Sugar-coating Error

Discussing concerns verbally isn't enough. Problems develop when supervisors talk at length about needs for improvement and other concerns, but just jot down a few general lines on the appraisal form itself. Everything communicated verbally should also appear in writing and vice versa. If not, and need for further action occurs, the available documentation falls short. Irene, for example, may consistently give incorrect information to other departments. But her appraisal reads only, "more care is needed in communicating to others." That does not cover the full scope of concern.

Recency of Events Error

Alleviating this error is one excellent reason for ensuring ongoing documentation and discussion. Without these activities, raters can forget the last five months of behavior and evaluate just the past five weeks. Employees sometimes exploit this reality, becoming especially active and visible just prior to a performance review. It's important to appraise the entire review period and not evaluate only the last portion of it, especially because it's so easy to forget incidents that could matter at review time, especially the positive ones. Even if a supervisor documents effectively, employees will benefit from carrying a "picture" of their efforts during the review cycle into the appraisal meeting, particularly if growth is shown from the prior cycle. It's not unusual for even HR directors to report that their direct reports go into high gear during the last quarter of the performance cycle.

Critical Incidents Effect

Similar to the halo and horns effects, this error distorts the overall review by giving undue emphasis to a single episode whether positive or negative. No one incident should predominate the entire review cycle. An especially glowing or poor performance at any point in the cycle should not serve to sweep the rest of the cycle under its influence.

Contrast Effect

When the evaluation of one employee affects that of another, it's known as a contrast error. Because every employee merits an appraisal based on individual performance, the contrast error skews the process. If a stellar performer, for example, is evaluated just before a good performer, the contrast might demote the second employee to just a fair rating. A contrast error can also result when the rater compares past and present performance. An employee rated good in one review might be rated poor in the next one, even though her performance could justifiably be rated as fair.

Personal Bias Error

Bias has many faces—and none belong in the appraisal. Some are readily apparent. But others are subtler, such as what is referred to as a similarity error. This distortion occurs when a supervisor gives a higher rating to an employee simply because they share similar characteristics. A supervisor may be totally unaware that he or she is even doing this. Long-time employees should be evaluated based on the quality of their performance, not on the number of years they have been with an organization. Ongoing careful documentation, coupled with objective standards goes a long distance toward countering a bias error. Stereotyping, or generalizing across a group, is tied to bias. Just as other forms of bias, stereotypical views can also be subtle. Not recognizing individual differences and assuming, for example, that all marketing directors are motivated and ambitious and that every engineer is highly analytical creates subjective standards from which rating errors might be drawn. There may also be perceptual difference errors shaped by the experiences and perspectives of the evaluators. An employee problem might be viewed subjectively within the evaluator's frame of reference rather than according to the realities of the employee's situation. A teacher, for example, might be appraised based on the rater's classroom experiences rather than on his own teaching skills.

Low Motivation Error

Evidence shows that it is more difficult to obtain accurate appraisals when important rewards depend on the results.[10] When the stakes are high, supervisors may be reluctant to provide an unbiased appraisal for fear of hurting the employee's chances of receiving added compensation, a promotion, or other opportunity for professional growth.

Past Anchoring Errors

Employees get caught in this error when managers rate performances based on prior evaluations instead of taking a fresh look.

Sampling Error

This error occurs when the evaluator appraises on the basis of just a small sample of an employee's work. With only a glimpse of output, the rating covers a complete review cycle.

Varying Standards Error

When two or more employees perform similar work, yet are held to different standards, the discrepancy distorts a fair and just evaluation process. One employee, for example, might be rated "good" for closing 65 percent of her sales while another employee documenting the identical number of closings is rated only as "fair."

Holding Employees Accountable When It's Not Their Fault

Widespread negative evaluations probably mean that fault is with management, not all of the employees being held accountable. If, for example, documents from large numbers of staff tend to show up late at certain times, the problem may be with technology. It's important know the differnece.

Employees should also not be held accountable for work requirements they were never told about, a problem that can surface when work standards are set without referring to the job description and actual requirements. This error is tied closely to the unrealistic objectives error, which holds employees accountable for work they're not trained for, fielding multiple priorities with unrealistic deadlines, completing complex assignments without adequate research assistance, and other such misplaced goals.

Attribution Bias

Distorted ratings occur when outstanding performance is "attributed" to factors external to the employee being rated, such as "great team support," but poor performance is perceived as being the outcome of an employee's own behavior. Poor technological acumen, for example, might be attributed to lack of employee understanding while organizational training might be credited when skills are excellent. In one instance, the employee is held accountable; in the second an external factor gains the praise. A supervisor may want to grab credit for good performance. When work goes well, it's because of good management. When it doesn't, it's due to poor employee performance.

Downsizing Rating Errors

Management Review

Performance appraisals should be reviewed by the manager's manager or Human Resources—and before sitting down with the employee. This is a good practice for ensuring that ratings match the narrative, and that the overall assessment is justified. The manager's manager is one-step removed and can contribute the objective insight and constructive feedback key to making necessary changes. The management review factors in safeguards that are important to both supervisor and organization.

■ ■ ■ ■ ■ ■ ■ ■ ■ ■ ■ ■

Checks & Balances

▣ Conduct rater training.

▣ Be clear about sequence of evaluation procedures.

▣ Ensure that supervisor's supervisor signs off on all appraisals—upfront.

▣ Build in time for HR to do a second check.

▣ Provide clear form inviting employee to respond in writing to review.

▣ Institute a formal appeals review, including a mediator if employee desires one.

■ ■ ■ ■ ■ ■ ■

Training

"Research shows that training can minimize rating errors. When raters learned which data to focus on, how to interpret it, and how to use it to formulate judgments, ratings were more reliable and accurate than when there was no training or training incongruent with rating needs."[11] The two most popular types of training programs are designed to help eliminate the kinds of errors previously described and to improve supervisors' observation and recording skills. While programs dealing with errors seem to eliminate many of them from ratings, there is much less evidence that this kind of training actually increases the accuracy of appraisals. Programs focused on observation and recording skills may offer greater improvements in accuracy than those that simply focus on errors.[12]

Regardless of the format, effective training spans full understanding of the evaluation process. It involves learning how to complete all materials, becoming a true player in appraisal sessions, being alert to legal implications, and leaving the door open to a continuing process. While trainers design sessions reflecting the particular culture and needs of organizations, there are workshop activities that successfully tackle the tough challenge of reducing rating errors.

Rater training serves to remind supervisors and employees of the importance of the appraisal process. It serves to underscore that for every employee to receive the fairest rating possible, information must be reviewed responsibly, knowledgeably, and legally. Because it's not too difficult for rating errors to creep into any performance evaluation, it's essential to be on guard against any distortion to the process.

Bottom-line, training will work only if supervisors are motivated and committed to applying it, and organizational accountability is built into the process. Conducting quality, timely performance appraisals should, in fact, be a rating classification in the appraisals of supervisors.

■■■■■■■■■■■■

Would you catch these rating errors?

1. Everyone in Stan's family is a scientist, so he's certainly smart enough to be learning faster. He deserves a poor rating.

2. From the day she walked in here, Mary's been so friendly to everyone. She's doing a great job. Her rating will be excellent.

3. Carol can process benefit claims faster than anyone. She has forgotten to share new procedures a few times and that's created errors and the need to reprocess. But she's fast and that's important so I'm giving her an overall high rating.

4. Margaret's desk is a mess. There's no way she can be clear about what she's doing. Her work has to suffer even though I can't recall any examples. A low rating will get her attention.

5. Gloria's work product is better than Wayne's. But they have to work together and I don't want to create a problem. I'll just rate Gloria a bit lower—right where Wayne is. That will motivate her and keep him happy.

6. I was a big hit at the director's retreat because Bernie did such a terrific job of pulling the presentation together. But since I did give him most of the materials, I'll grade him "average" for his efforts.

7. It's so comfortable being with Sheridan. She's new and there have been a few mistakes. Some really surprised me. But talking with her is like being with a sister. She's a super addition to this office and I want to recognize that.

8. Roger is exceptionally creative but he doesn't follow process. He generates ideas and starts working before management even signs off. I'll talk with him about it, but only include a line stating that he "needs to work more methodically" in his appraisal so he's not hurt and I don't come across as too permissive.

1.	Stereotyping	5.	Central tendency error
2.	Halo effect	6.	Attribution bias
3.	Leniency error	7.	Personal bias
4.	Harshness error	8.	Sugar-coating and sunflower effect

■ ■ ■ ■ ■ ■ ■

Appeals Process

Most companies build an employee response step into the appraisal process, giving employees an opportunity to express their reaction. This may take the form of an employee-generated memo, but often it is an official response form that is attached to the appraisal. Sometimes happy employees will respond accordingly. More common are the responses from employees who are displeased with their ratings. These employees are more apt to express their reaction. A number of organizations make sure these employees have another option—a complaint resolution process or formal grievance procedure. Smart companies believe that any employee with a complaint should have the opportunity to be heard and have the concern promptly and objectively reviewed and corrected, if necessary, with no fear of retaliation. Organizations support resolution through varying routes. Some are two- or three-step processes. Others are more extensive.

For any process to be effective, it should include an orderly and well-communicated system, specific steps and time frames that are followed by any employee with a similar issue. Conflict resolution processes begin with an employee putting his or her rebuttal in writing, then discussing concerns with the immediate supervisor. The organization should designate in writing how many days the employee has to schedule and conduct this meeting, and each subsequent meeting as necessary.

If the issue is not yet resolved, a more formal process begins. At this point, an independent mediator might be brought into the process. The aim is to facilitate a resolution as quickly as possible. If the employee remains dissatisfied, the supervisor can schedule a private meeting between the employee and the supervisor's supervisor. Again, this meeting should occur within a certain time frame, after which both managers write the results of their respective meetings on designated portions of the appraisal form. If an employee still seeks a resolution, the employee can meet with the next level of management. That individual looks into the matter and proposes a solution.

If still unsettled, a panel of trained peers can review the evidence of both employee and supervisor. Guided by a mediator, panelists can conduct a meeting during which they will explore information from both parties. The peers will make a decision within organizational parameters. Human Resources and one of the highest officers (or equivalent) will review the panel's decision, either signing off on the decision and making it binding or offering an alternative solution that all parties can live with.

Three Scenarios

Scenarios about Marilyn, Richard, and Peg demonstrate the ease with which rating errors can occur. A generally high performer, Marilyn gets along well with everyone. As a result, her supervisor gives her an across-the-board excellent rating without first reviewing results pertinent to the full range of rating categories. **(halo effect)** As another example, one of Marilyn's key responsibilities during the appraisal cycle was to contract out construction designed to expand the office in time for new attorneys to come on board. Despite contractor delays, Marilyn made sure the job was accomplished on deadline. As significant as it was, her supervisor allowed this one achievement to color all others. **(critical incidents effect)**

Richard's mother was rushed to the hospital two weeks prior to his performance review. Unexpectedly away from the office, he never transitioned his work and part of an important assignment slipped through the cracks. This incident stayed fresh in the mind of his supervisor, who gave him an overall low performance rating despite other positive outcomes during the appraisal cycle. **(recency of events error)** In another instance, Richard's duplicating department budget was sliced despite a commitment to produce work for a client requiring technology now placed on hold. Told to deliver anyway, Richard needed to outsource the work, then was held responsible for the budget deficit. **(unrealistic objectives error)**

Despite continuing poor performance, Peg's supervisor keeps trying to support her, postponing or derailing the need to fire her. She's also concerned that a poor rating will affect her own supervisor's view of her as a manager. The result is that Peg's review is generally higher than merited, which does not serve Peg, her supervisor, or the advertising agency where they work. **(sunflower effect)**

■ ■ ■ ■ ■ ■ ■ ■ ■ ■ ■ ■

Exercises for Large and Small Groups

Open by asking participants to generate a list of why performance appraisals are important—this jump-starts thinking about long-term importance *before* focusing on the form. Ask what documentation is needed to arrive at a fair rating, including last year's goals, significant accomplishments, job description, work examples, observation notes, input from others, employee's self-assessment, and any other job- or goal-related information based on performance that should not be overlooked. Build a discussion about the value and pitfalls of each item.

Stage a role-play in which an "employee" works through each section of the evaluation form, with ratings based on examples drawn from the previously mentioned material. The "employee" challenges the ratings, providing the "supervisor" a chance to clarify why and how ratings were conceived. Sprinkled through the explanation are blatant, then subtler examples of rating errors. Participants have sheets listing many rating errors. Individually, then as a group, they are identified.

Small group exercises are useful, too. After a general explanation of rating errors, written scenarios are distributed and participants break into small groups to identify the source of problems. The larger group can then convene to discuss reactions to the process of identifying, then correcting errors. As a group, there can be discussion of what supervisors and employees can best do to spot rating errors before they take hold.

※ ※ ※ ※ ※ ※

When Appraisals Go Off Track

7

Tell me, I will forget,
Show me, I may remember,
Involve me, I will understand

—Chinese Proverb

Perhaps the appraisal discussion derails. That can occur when there have been no mini-reviews with checks and balances along the way. If employees haven't initiated feedback, and their supervisors haven't offered it, substantial misunderstandings can result. Then the yearly review hits, and there is the potential to blow a lot of good will. In which case, add another quote, "Blessed are the flexible, for they shall not be bent out of shape!"[1]

This is the time for what author Jim Collins calls an "autopsy without blame,"[2] an open, honest look at the reasons for derailment and their root causes "in a climate where the truth can be heard."[3] Such an environment requires not just hearing but "active listening." On the supervisor's part, it requires a clear explanation of purpose, a willingness to establish trust, the openness to invite the employee into the feedback process, and a genuine effort to understand what the employee is saying. Feedback must be treated as information, not as a value judgment.[4] On the employee's part, it takes much of the same, with demonstrated willingness to not just hang in but to become actively engaged in owning the appraisal. For both supervisor and employee, there is that "A list"—being active, accurate, attentive, and appreciative (Chapter 2). As described earlier, mainstreaming these four values into the supervisor/employee relationship gives a terrific boost to positive on-the-job experiences. If these values were rampant, there would be no need for this chapter. Or to conduct as many autopsies.

Every autopsy, of course, is conducted through the lens of perception. "Everything is a matter of perception, even perceptions themselves...Change people's perceptions and you change the game. Shaping perceptions is the domain of tactics, those actions [people] take to shape the perceptions of others. Some tactics are designed to lift a fog, others to preserve a fog and yet others to stir up a new fog."[5] This chapter aims to lift the fog. There is no value here in Harry Truman's quip: "If you can't convince them, confuse them."

In *Co-opetition*, Adam M. Brandenburger and Barry J. Nalebuff wrote that, "Intentional or not, everything you do sends a signal to others. For the same reason, everything you don't do sends a signal to others, too."[6] Whether active or passive, verbal or, even more importantly, nonverbal, these signals are the stuff of perception. And it's perceptions that drive our behavior.

Perceptions don't even need to be accurate. Just being alive in a person's frame of reference is all that's needed. In his landmark research, Dov Eden described how this can play out at work. Perceptions shape expectations, and Eden showed that managers' expectations can have a powerful effect on the quality and productivity of their employees' work. They can, in fact, create a self-fulfilling prophecy. Eden asked: "To what extent do the expectations of a manager affect his or her evaluation of an employee, and to what extent does this evaluation communicate a manager's expectations to that employee, and thereby shape the employee's future performance?" His findings: positive expectations influence managers' perceptions and evaluations of employee behavior positively, and negative expectations have adverse effects.[7] Which, of course, only reinforces existing perceptions.

"Fear Is That Little Dark Room Where Negatives Are Developed"

When an appraisal derails, chances are high that negative perceptions are already on the table. The challenge is to find out why—without becoming entangled in a way that adds to the problem. While it's often tough to feel positive in a difficult situation, the pay-off is worth it. There is already an investment in the work and the working relationship. If the relationship is to continue, it needs to work well. In the previous quote, motivational speaker Michael Pritchard recognized that below negativity lies fear.

Cutting through the fear is a process, not the first step. "The first step in a coaching process is to gain agreement that a problem exists. This first step is where managers fail in their efforts to eliminate performance problems. They fail here because they bypass it."[8] There are two reasons that convince problem performers there is a problem:

1. When they understand the results to the organization of what they are doing wrong or failing to do right.

2. When they understand the consequences to themselves if there is no change in performance.

Ninety-five percent of nonperformers will agree there is a problem once they recognize the results of what they are doing wrong. Ninety-five percent of that remaining five percent will agree there is a problem once they recognize the consequences to themselves of not stopping it. People don't usually self-destruct on purpose.[9]

Agreeing there is a problem opens the door to identifying it. Perhaps the employee doesn't know what is expected, or doesn't know how to deliver. Maybe the necessary resources aren't in place. Or the employee just isn't interested. There may be outside issues.

■ ■ ■ ■ ■ ■ ■ ■ ■ ■ ■ ■

How to Trust Your Boss

- ▣ Understand your boss's personality, management, and work style.
- ▣ Communicate with him/her in a way that's most effective.
- ▣ Find out what the boss's expectations are.
- ▣ Get a clear picture of the boss's job, goals, priorities, and pressures.
- ▣ Avoid making the boss look bad.
- ▣ Keep him/her informed; avoid surprises.
- ▣ Trust your boss and be trustworthy.
- ▣ Give him/her the benefit of the doubt.

- Be supportive.
- Be loyal.
- Assume responsibility.
- Produce quality work.
- Respect the person's need for privacy.

■ ■ ■ ■ ■ ■ ■

Deep feelings may be involved, usually tapping into fears described in Chapter 1. "There are situations in which our most cherished views, our most steadfast attitudes, and our most deeply felt emotions are challenged and threatened. There are cases when the total semantic transactor that we have become feels we have either to assert ourselves or accept a crushing defeat. To entertain the possibility of a compromise seems impossible; it would be like a shameful abdication of self-respect. There surges within us a survival call for all the resources of native resiliency and acquired skill we can muster in what appears to be a life or death emergency."[10] In such cases, feelings may run hot at the appraisal table.

Important principles may also be at stake. These need to be heeded. "People should do the right thing, not half of it. They should tell the whole truth, not half-truths. They should be fair all the time, not just on Mondays, Wednesdays or Fridays. Like the baby brought to Solomon, moral principles seem to be invisible. They should be defended, with courage and determination, not haggled away."[11]

"Messy, Everyday Challenges"

More often the vast majority of problems are everyday situations. They aren't labeled strategic or critical, but what Joseph C. Badaracci, in his bestseller, *Leading Quietly*, calls "messy everyday challenges." "Anyone can face these challenges at almost any time. Hard choices don't involve 'time out' from everyday life, but are embedded in its very fabric."[12] That, of course, includes work life.

Getting an appraisal discussion back on track means both parties genuinely seek a workable solution. Even if not comfortable initially, there is the respectful willingness to derive understanding from each other's perceptions, and to arrive at workable solutions. Ideally, there is a cultural mindset in your organization that fosters this approach. If not, a supervisor and employee can elevate the standards, at least for their own comfort and their department's productivity. Creating a climate where truth is heard can be characterized by four basic practices:

1. Lead with questions, not answers.

2. Engage in dialogue and debate, not coercion.

3. Conduct autopsies without blame.

4. Build red flag mechanisms that turn information into information that cannot be ignored.[13]

■ ■ ■ ■ ■ ■ ■ ■ ■ ■ ■ ■

Respect the other person's opinion or stance.

Empathize with the other person's position; be at ease with expressing your own.

Share interests that can lead to common ground; they always exist when there's an openness to embrace them.

Understand the difference between a person and an issue.

Listen actively to information and solutions.

Treat the other person respectfully.

■ ■ ■ ■ ■ ■ ■

Inherent in continuing efforts is the conviction that the employee can, in fact, do what is needed. He or she has the choice to move ahead on a positive track—with the demonstrated understanding that the supervisor is on board as well. People may think that conditions determine choices when, in fact, it's often the opposite. Far more often it's the choices themselves that create the path [that] follows.[14]

In *Coaching*, Ferdinand F. Fournies emphasized that, "It's important to remember that this is a discussion: two people are participating in a conversation."[15] Supervisors shouldn't be lecturing or answering their own questions. Fournies pointed out that "employees have learned that if the boss asks them a question and they don't answer it, the boss answers his or her own question." If, after a reasonable period, the employee still hasn't answered, the supervisor can ask if the employee wants the question repeated.[16]

In working toward next steps, Fournies cautioned against "combining the selection of alternatives with the listing or discovery of alternatives. These are two clearly separate functions: combining them inhibits the optimum achievement of either. If you argue the merits of ideas as they are given, you are wasting *idea-giving time.* If you reject ideas as they are given, you could be punishing *idea-giving behavior,* thereby decreasing the behavior of idea giving. The process of generating ideas depends on the interaction of ideas,"[17] and the process needs patience to most effectively run its course. The best ideas may even rebound from the bad or seemingly trivial ones. [18]

"Successful negotiation engages people, especially those who have ongoing interaction, in seeking and identifying a solution satisfactory to all. When both sides are open to winning on some points and compromising or losing on others, they are more likely to arrive at a solution they can accept and support. When a clear winner and a clear loser emerge from a negotiation session, hard feelings are likely to result. The "loser" may undermine the solution, and it is possible that no one will 'win' in the long run."[19]

Supervisor: *It's time to start the inventory count next week.*

Employee: *I created a new system for us to use.*

Supervisor: *I'm not convinced...I've been using our old system for years.*

Employee: *It has some great features I think you'll like and it lets us get the job done quicker.*

Supervisor: *Let's do this...continue to use the old tracking forms but add the new columns for the extra data you're gathering. We can review it together and decide how to proceed. Sound fair?*

■■■■■■■■■■■■

Blueprint for Positive Appraisals

▣ Give feedback that is specific and behavioral.

▣ Describe the behavior's impact on the team or the attainment of the person's goals.

▣ Express your observations calmly.

▣ Avoid overwhelming the person with too much feedback all at once.

- Let the person present his or her side of the problem, engage in a dialogue, and avoid any tendency to lecture.

- Focus on the future.

- Clearly identify the pay-off.

- Provide the appropriate balance of positive and negative feedback. Offer to help improve.

- Express empathy when you perceive discouragement. Acknowledge that change does not happen overnight and can be difficult.

■ ■ ■ ■ ■ ■ ■

"People are *up* on things they're in on."[20] Open communication fosters trust, so be candid. If you tend to sit on things, commit during the appraisal to begin following the 24-hour rule, which means creating opportunities to talk about concerns without dodging them. Be as inclusive in your discussion as possible. Just as straight talk increases trust, trust increases ownership, and ownership increases participation.[21]

The Successful Manager's Handbook presents seven ways to open communication and five ways to field disagreement:[22]

1. Let people know in a timely way about information that affects them. Respond as quickly as possible to their questions.

2. Be aware of sending nonverbal messages. Communicate a positive, face-to-face message. Make eye contact, or use other culturally appropriate gestures.

3. Convey positive, constructive feedback. Positive feedback lets people know the behavior you appreciate.

4. Constructive feedback informs people of ineffective behavior, providing the opportunity to improve.

5. If conflicting, mixed messages come up, confront the discrepancy and work to clarify the misunderstanding.

6. When you receive vague messages, define the issues concretely so that both parties are clear about what is being said.

7. To get a point across in a direct, nonaggressive fashion, simply say what you think and feel without putting the other person down.

When someone disagrees with you:

1. Wait until the person has finished speaking, even if you're sure you understand the argument.

2. Restate the main points of the person's viewpoint and then really try to understand his or her perspective.

3. Ask the person to verify the accuracy of your restatement and to clarify if necessary.

4. Identify those points or goals with which you sincerely agree.

5. Only then, state what you disagree with, and explain why.

"Write People's Accomplishments in Stone and Their Faults in the Sand."

In large part, perceptions are shaped by the signals we send, and all of us send signals all the time. In an anxiety-provoking situation, these signals, verbal and nonverbal, can either exacerbate an already tense situation or considerably tone it down. The previous quote, by Benjamin Franklin, lends an approach that works well in discussing derailed appraisals. It's not meant to let employees off the hook, just to offer a safe harbor for nurturing openness and trust.

Verbally and nonverbally, messages should be supportive. "Ask yourself: Do I want my message to be heard defensively, or accurately? Is it my purpose to hurt someone, to aggrandize myself, or to communicate?"[23] Given that words and approaches can build or destroy, it's critical to communicate with care, using several other questions as a checklist:

❑ Do you choose your words with care?

❑ Do you check for understanding?

❑ Do you speak clearly?

❑ Do you concentrate on what is being said?

❑ Do you avoid interrupting the speaker?

❑ Do you acknowledge that you understand?

❑ Do you withhold judgment?

❑ Do you allow others to speak?

Nature seems to favor the positive. "It takes an average person almost twice as long to understand a sentence that uses a negative approach [instead of] a positive sentence."[24] And because "the mind thinks at least six times faster than we can speak,"[25] perceptions are well into play before the employee or supervisor has completed even one sentence! That's why really listening and asking for feedback to ensure that words and meanings are clear can make a dramatic and positive difference. Because any misunderstanding can be a springboard for an inaccurate perception, it's critical to correct it before the inaccurate perception takes hold and subsequently feeds other ones.

Natalie Loeb, a New Jersey performance development consultant, calls feedback a gift. "It's hard," she says, "to correct something when you're not clear what it is."

Employee: *I know why you called me in.*

Supervisor: *Why do you think?*

Employee: *I came in late again yesterday. It's that bus. It always runs late.*

Supervisor: *Yes, Jessica, I am concerned about that. But the real problem is that we have a team here. You're on the team. If you can come in late, it's not fair to the others. The same thing applies to the weekly report. I depend on everyone's feedback to move it to the board. So do you see what the problem really is here?*

Employee: *I'm not sure.*

Supervisor: *I want to hear what you think.*

Employee: *I guess I need to be more on time with things.*

Supervisor: *Why do you think?*

Employee: *I'm part of the whole team here. And I'm creating holes.*

Supervisor: *You say it well, Jessica. Can I count on you now to fill them?*

Employee: *I'm on board.*

To get the appraisal discussion back on track, both employees and supervisors should carefully scrutinize their analyses to make certain it's coming from objective, documented conclusions rather than personal intolerance.[26] "This is [the] chance to mutually generate creative options...don't blow it by imposing solutions."[27] Supportive messages steer clear of these following destructive tactics:[28]

- 回 **Global labels.** Hurtful words indict the total person rather than provide commentary on a specific behavior.

- 回 **Sarcasm.** Usually contemptuous, this brand of humor covers anger and hurt.

- 回 **Dragging up the past.** Raking over old wounds diverts from focus on the present.

- 回 **Negative comparisons.** Comparisons are deadly, serving only to convey that someone is inferior.

- 回 **Judgmental "you" messages.** These serve simply to accuse.

- 回 **Threats.** Guaranteed to bring meaningful communication to a halt.

In her writing, Deborah Tannen, widely published author and linguistics professor at Georgetown University in Washington, D.C., called attention to "some typical ways the conversational signals of pacing, pausing, loudness, and pitch are used to carry on the business of taking turns in conversation; relating ideas to each other and showing what the point is; and showing how we feel about what we're saying and about the person we're saying it to. These are the signals that combine with what is said to make up the devices we use to show we're listening, interested, sympathetic, or teasing—and that we're the right sort of people. Normally invisible, these conversational signals and devices are the silent and hidden gears that drive conversation."[29] "We don't pay attention to these gears unless something seems to have gone wrong," Tannen wrote. "Then we may ask, 'What do you *mean* by that?' And even then we don't think in terms of the signals—'Why did your pitch go up?'—but in terms of intentions—'Why are you angry?'"

Derailed appraisals can represent a struggle to say what we mean. But "Say what you mean, and mean what you say" is only half of it. How the information is taken in, and what occurs in the translation is where trip-ups also occur. This is especially true if blocks to listening are in play.

■ ■ ■ ■ ■ ■ ■ ■ ■ ■ ■ ■

Listening Blocks[30]

Comparing: Assessing while you're hearing precludes listening.

Mind-reading: Mind-readers tend to assume, distrusting what is being said.

Rehearsing: Preparing doesn't allow time to listen.

Filtering: Selective listening means your mind is wandering.

Judging: This is fine, once all content is heard and evaluated.

Dreaming: Half listening indicates little value for what is being said.

Identifying: It's hard to listen when you're caught up in your own experience.

Advising: Being too ready to help limits listening time.

Sparring: Too much debating and too little listening make people feel unheard.

Being Right: Active listening might shake up your "unshakeable" convictions...and correct help mistakes.

Derailing: Joking or veering away from a topic squashes the other person's interest.

Placating: *Right...Right...Absolutely...* is listening halfway without genuine involvement.

■ ■ ■ ■ ■ ■ ■

■ ■ ■ ■ ■ ■ ■ ■ ■ ■ ■ ■

Undoing Destructive Supervisory Styles[31]

Attacker: Cite employee's specific behaviors and their effects, then opportunities to improve.

Judge: Share only objective accounts of the employee's behavior. Avoid loaded language ("bad" or "lazy").

Rambler: Keep it short and simple and describe current behavior.

Hit and Run: *Actively* listen. Get full story. Share ideas.

Dumper: Provide feedback gradually, in a single context.

Laggard: Give feedback when it most counts—immediately!

Inconsiderate: Present feedback at appropriate time, *only* with employee involved.

Fabricator: Base information on direct observations and solid documentation. Quantify when possible.

Parent: Select a few consequences that will get employee's attention—and tie to organizational interests.

Punisher: Keep focus positive, even with negative impacts.

Psychologist: Openly discuss ways to avoid future problems. Be cautious of "whys."

Imposer: Recognize it's employee's responsibility to come up with alternatives, and be more committed to his or her plans.

Abandoner: Create a plan and stay on top of it. Be supportive.

Quick Fixer: Brainstorm alternatives.

Pessimist: Be positive—and mean it!

■ ■ ■ ■ ■ ■ ■

The Hostile Employee

Toni, the front office desk clerk, doesn't accept responsibility for substandard performance and gets very angry and defensive during the appraisal discussion. She disagrees with her review and blames other employees while speaking with her supervisor, Lydia.

TIPS

- **Let Toni respond.**
- **Listen.**
- **Ask Toni questions to find out the real reason for her anger.**

Lydia:	*It's time to discuss a few areas where you can concentrate some additional effort.*
Toni:	*What are you talking about?*
Lydia:	*Well, I have a few samples of the monthly reports here. There are some gaps where room charges needed to be added before you submitted them.*
Toni:	*Just a minute. That wasn't my fault!*

Lydia: *Tell me how you think the process failed. Is there something else bothering you?*

- **Restate your point of view.**
- **Let Toni know that it is difficult to continue the conversation with so much emotion.**

Lydia: *Toni, I'd like to do some problem-solving with you here.*

Toni: *I think you're just trying to blame me. You know very well that the kitchen staff is responsible for getting that information to me. Why should I have to remind them when it's due? They're adults! You just want to criticize me.*

Lydia: *I don't want to criticize you. I want you to be the best employee around here.*

Toni: *Right.*

- **Decide if it is prudent to continue the performance appraisal meeting.**
- **If not, reschedule. If possible, establish some ground rules for the rest of the meeting and continue.**

Lydia: *Toni, I can see that you're upset. These discussions about performance are not meant to do that. Why don't we meet again later this afternoon, 3 p.m., and we'll start over? I'll expect you to approach the topic of work problems constructively. And we'll both come to that meeting with some solutions. Is that a deal?*

- **Be ready to share with Toni examples that support the ratings and/or narrative comments on the performance appraisal form.**
- **Let Toni know that you will give her resources to help her in her work and be available to provide guidance.**
- **Make sure she understands that she will be responsible for her performance. If she is able to turn things around, you will be her biggest supporter.**

The Too-Quiet Employee

Joe, the mail clerk, accepts the review without saying a word and prepares to leave before there has been much discussion. The review is very fair and balanced, overall acceptable, or so Charlie, his supervisor, thinks. It seems that Joe is agreeing with the supervisor to either end the session quickly or to please the supervisor.

TIPS

- **Probe to see what Joe's feelings are.**
- **Make sure he understands the performance issues.**
- **Ask open-ended questions to encourage him to talk.**

Charlie: *I've covered all the points I wanted to go over with you, Joe, but you haven't said much. I was hoping for more of a two-way conversation about your performance.*

Joe: *Well...*

Charlie: *Why don't you give me your reaction to what I've said.*

Joe: *It was all fine, Charlie, really. I agree.*

Charlie: *Okay. Let's talk about some future projects for you. What would interest you?*

Joe: *Whatever you want me to focus on is fine with me. You're the boss, Charlie.*

- **Tell Joe that he will be expected to talk 60 percent of the meeting time.**
- **Listen.**
- **Allow silences.**
- **Reschedule, if necessary.**

Charlie: *No, Joe, that's not how this works. This is your performance appraisal, a discussion pulling together all the quick talks we've had over the last six months. It's time for reflection, for planning, and for some good feedback, both ways. Maybe I wasn't clear about what I hoped this meeting could achieve. Why don't we reschedule for tomorrow morning and we'll pick up there. I'll expect you to do most of the talking, Joe, so be ready. Give some thought as to what you'd like to do next quarter during the remodeling of the mailroom. Remember, Joe, I'm going to do a lot of listening, not talking. See you then.*

- **Have more frequent meetings with Joe.**

The New Supervisor

Tara was recently brought in from the outside to be the Senior VP of Human Resources. Lucas, Director of Employee Relations, wanted that position and felt he was qualified. He was very disappointed that he wasn't selected and has not accepted Tara in her role as his supervisor.

TIPS

- **Anticipate resistance.**
- **Respect feelings.**
- **Be patient.**
- **Avoid confrontation or downplaying conflict; try to refuse resistance.**
- **Give adjustment time.**
- **Show yourself as a supportive boss; remain positive.**

  Tara: *It's time to have your performance appraisal, Lucas.*

  Lucas: *Well, you haven't been here long enough to assess my work.*

  Tara: *That's true. So I won't be doing a full appraisal at this time. But I wanted to share the form your prior supervisor left. However, as we work together in the months ahead, I'll be able to see the good work you do firsthand. I'm looking forward to it.*

- **Stress common ground/areas of agreement; build rapport.**
- **Be clear about expectations.**
- **Stress mutual benefits for department.**

  Tara: *I know we both want to be involved in the most effective and efficient HR operation. And I think we could make a formidable team. I'd like us to set some reachable goals for you and your group for the next quarter. Let's examine the turnover statistics and supervisory training sessions for the last year. I'd like your thoughts on how we can reduce the number of unemployment claims and terminations.*

  Lucas: *I have a lot of ideas.*

  Tara: *Great. I was hoping you would. Let's get started. This will be the first in a series of meetings for us.*

- **Keep communication open. Cultivate the relationship.**

The Settled-in Employee

Harvey, the copywriter, has been a long-term employee who has not received honest feedback regarding his performance for years. Dorinne, his new supervisor, has taken her responsibility of preparing an honest appraisal very conscientiously and has to review some areas of unsatisfactory and marginal performance. Dorinne has tried to provide open and honest feedback throughout the performance period but Harvey refuses to hear it.

TIPS

- **Show appreciation for the value Harvey adds.**
- **Ask Harvey how he thinks things are going. His responses may help Dorinne decide how to proceed.**
- **Give specific examples of his performance that fell short of expectations.**
- **Review a few earlier conversations regarding his performance.**

Dorinne: *Harvey, you've been with the department quite awhile and you've seen a lot of changes. I rely on you to give me some of that archival knowledge you have on so many projects. I value that. As we discussed through the year, there are a few areas that need some attention.*

Harvey: *With all due respect, Dorinne, you're my fifth supervisor in seven years and everyone else thought I was doing just fine.*

Dorinne: *I can't comment on how others might have evaluated your work, Harvey. But I need you to know that I take this responsibility quite seriously. I want to continue to give you honest feedback to help you be even more of an asset to our unit. I think there are some things we can work on together. I'd like that. For example, I have some ideas that might help you get your response rate up. Your last three packages didn't meet the target.*

- **Restate expectations.**
- **Ask open-ended questions to determine how Harvey feels about his job.**
- **Reinforce his strengths.**
- **Develop a plan for improvement together.**

- **Express support that Harvey can meet the expectations.**
- **Establish a follow up process.**

    Dorinne: *I've gotten the conference schedule for the copywriters' seminar next month. Perhaps a few of the technical sessions would be helpful. You need to get your response rate up to 10 percent. Which sessions might be most helpful, do you think? I know you'll be able to bump up those numbers. Let's review the next package together, okay?*

The Surprise Appraisal

Paul is a "hands-off" director rarely available to his manager, Bernie. It's now time for the performance appraisal meeting and Bernie has no idea what Paul will say. There has been no ongoing dialog throughout the performance period and Bernie is looking forward to some constructive feedback.

TIPS (for the employee)

- **Don't expect too much.**
- **Actively solicit feedback.**
- **Hit the high points of your performance; be brief and focused. Don't be long-winded; don't overwhelm.**
- **Present a well-documented self-appraisal.**
- **Get clarification on expectations.**

    Paul: *You're doing fine, Lou, just fine.*

    Bernie: *Thanks, Paul. I've been looking forward to hearing more about how I'm doing.*

    Paul: *More?*

    Bernie: *Well, details about what I did that really worked, what I could have improved on. And of course, future projects....*

    Paul: *I see.*

    Bernie: *I've prepared a self-appraisal for you to check. I've highlighted my major responsibilities at the top, along with some of the major projects for the last six months. Could we briefly go through that?*

- **Read clues as to when Paul is ready for the meeting to end.**

    Bernie: *Two last questions because I know you need to get to another meeting. Do you have specific deliverables for me next quarter? And what specifically would you advise me to do to get ready for my next step professionally? I value your opinion. I'd be available to pick up this discussion later if that works better for you. These meetings help me so much.*

- **Accept that details aren't important to Paul.**
- **Try for brief follow-up meetings in the future; express how helpful they are.**

Planning for Improvement

8

*Words mean more than what is set down on paper.
It takes the human voice to infuse them with deeper
meaning.*

—Maya Angelou, civil rights activist, poet,
and one of the greatest voices of
contemporary literature.

In managing performance, any bumps can usually be smoothed through the evaluation process and its continuing informal reviews and follow-up performance objectives. Most employees want to do a good job, and most employers are invested in their success. But sometimes this isn't enough. When performance continues to disintegrate, a Performance Improvement Plan (PIP) is warranted. PIPs can help make the difference between an effective and failing employee.

Based on the belief that, given the right opportunity, most employers and employees want to turn things around, the PIP is a written document aimed at measurable performance improvement. The goal is to help the employee reach an acceptable level of performance. By charting a clear course, with firm objectives and realistic steps for meeting them, the PIP creates a picture of success, an important morale booster for an employee whose work is substandard and is unclear what to do about it. The plan is a valuable management tool for supervisors grappling with a difficult performance problem.

PIPs are characterized by measurable standards, including the willingness to benefit from coaching, training and other assets. Milestone dates and progress points are built in. A completion date is set, and the consequences of meeting or not meeting expectations are explicit. Following up at specific junctures is key, and both supervisor and employee must be genuinely invested in producing positive results. Intent to commit to a PIP can be introduced by the supervisor and agreed to by the employee during the appraisal discussion. The next step is to develop the PIP, which should be given to an employee directly and discussed before implementation begins.

As emphasized in Chapter 2, solid documentation is critical. Every employee is entitled to equitable treatment and most supervisors want to give it. In developing PIPs, documentation is important, not only for accurate recall but to document a sequence of events. Don't depend on memory. Both supervisors and employees should document an occurrence soon as possible after it occurs, then double-check it for objectivity and accuracy. Establish a tracking system that eases documentation and is readily accessible. The amount of documentation can be determined by the issue, the frequency, and the impact.

■■■■■■■■■■■■

Sound Written PIPs Provide...

▣ Clear, accurate details about failing performance.

▣ Effects of situation.

▣ Standards that require change.

▣ Specific resources and other helpful suggestions.

▣ Milestone dates to assess progress in meeting goals.

▣ End date by which improvement is expected.

▣ Consequences of meeting or not meeting objectives.

▣ Employee's signature.

■ ■ ■ ■ ■ ■ ■

■■■■■■■■■■■■

Introducing a PIP

▣ Schedule a meeting free of distractions.

▣ Acknowledge willingness, on both sides, to commit to turning things around. State the performance problem.

▣ With a few examples, explain the effect of the problem (on others, the department, organization, or customers).

▣ Listen.

▣ Review the entire PIP.

▣ Based on employee feedback, adjust as necessary.

▣ Double-check that everything is clear, including the consequences of meeting or not meeting objectives.

▣ Set date for follow-up meeting.

▣ End on a positive, supportive note.

▣ Make clear that the employee can respond in writing and that the response will be attached to the PIP.

▣ Assure confidentiality.

At Completion Date

▣ Recognize employee for successfully meeting objectives.

▣ Review documentation with legal counsel to prepare for termination.

■ ■ ■ ■ ■ ■ ■

Following are three approaches to developing Performance Improvement Plans:

Peg, one of three people being tracked in this book, is clearly in job-jeopardy. She has performed poorly for several months. She arrives late and takes too many unscheduled days off. There is always a large pile of unfinished work on her desk. After several coaching sessions and a written warning in her file, there is still no improvement. The PIP is a last effort to save her job. Here's how the discussion about Peg's PIP might be presented and documented.

Confidential Memorandum to Peg and File

Today we met to discuss your performance for the review period (dates). During this meeting, I informed you that your overall performance rating for this period is: "Requires Improvement." You currently require improvement in managing time, communication, customer service, quality of work, and attendance.

As a result of receiving a "Required Improvement" performance rating, I have developed the following performance plan to help you improve your performance to an "Achieved Standards" level. Your performance improvement period will begin on (*date*) and end on (*date*). I have included weekly meeting dates to measure and discuss your progress toward the following objective and performance expectations. We will meet on (*date, date, date, date, and date*). You will receive feedback at these meetings, which will be followed up in writing.

An "Achieved Standards" level of performance will include:

Attendance

The ability to arrive at work at the agreed start time, 9 am, is essential. Your work schedule has been adjusted in the past to allow you more time for arrival, yet the adjusted time hasn't resolved the issue. As a result, you don't always work a full seven-hour day. Arriving at work by 9 am and requesting and obtaining approval for leave in advance will improve your attendance and allow staff members to plan projects according to your scheduled time off. Your irregular attendance has caused delays in completing projects (for example, last client mailing) and inaccuracies in many work products.

- **Arrive at work by 9 am and request and obtain approval for leave in advance.**
- **Depart work at 5 pm.**

Customer Service

Providing lead telephone reception for the department is a very visible responsibility that delivers a first impression of our agency. Timely fulfillment of client requests and prompt responses to telephone inquiries have suffered greatly in the past three months. For example, clients often indicate that they have not received requested items and materials from you. It is essential that you answer the phone in a prompt and courteous manner, responding to requests within 24 hours.

- **Answer the phone in a prompt and courteous manner, responding to requests within 24 hours.**

Quality of Work

Completing assignments within designated time frames and producing good quality work must be high priorities. Frequently, you have mailed letters with omissions and typographical and grammatical errors, specifically the marketing assignment letters and meeting invitations. You need to pay close attention to details. For example, proofreading assignments will help ensure that all pertinent information is included and that documents are grammatically correct. Using the spell check before finalizing and mailing documents will aid in improving the quality of your work. You are responsible for delivering a final work product that is accurate and free of errors.

- **Proofread assignments to be sure that all pertinent information is included, helping to ensure that documents are grammatically correct. Use the spell check before finalizing and mailing documents.**

Time Management and Communications

Handling multiple tasks simultaneously is a critical job function. Finding efficient ways to manage your time effectively, and organizing and prioritizing assignments (for example, creating client files and using automated reminders) can prevent important details from slipping. For example, when you did not follow up on the request for an AV projector for the presentation on (*date*), it was not delivered, causing a gap in the set-up for the meeting and an interruption once the equipment arrived. There have also been instances when you have mailed meeting materials to a site at the last minute, causing the materials to arrive late, or even after the session was over.

Working closely with other administrative staff to explore different methods of accomplishing tasks will be helpful and save time, particularly when you are unclear about how to proceed with a work project. Increased communications with staff, such as seeking clarity by asking questions when you are unsure of assignment specifications, will eliminate the need to duplicate work (for example, coupling preparation of the convention attendance list and mail merge letters). This will allow you to move forward with different projects.

- **Work closely with other administrative staff to explore different methods of accomplishing tasks.**
- **Seek clarity by asking questions when you are unsure of assignment specifications.**

- **Find efficient solutions to organize and prioritize assignments (for example, creating client files and using automated reminders) to assist you in completing projects within designated time frames and allow you time to move forward with other assignments.**
- **You should obtain the Self-Study Learning Tool, "Making Your Time Count," available from our Human Resources Department. This course demonstrates effective and practical time-management and self-management techniques that will help you better manage your time.**

Peg, the previous information represents the expectations that I have of you as a Receptionist. Please be advised that I am available to assist you in improving your performance in the areas previously outlined. I also want to remind you of the resources available to you as an employee. The Employee Assistance Program offers confidential, professional counseling and life management services to our employees and eligible family members and it can be reached at (*telephone number*).

I look forward to working with you during these next weeks. Again, I am available to answer any questions you may have or to provide you with any guidance you may require to improve your job performance. However, you should be aware that if you do not improve your performance to an "Achieved Standards" level by (*date*), or if you have not completed the previously-outlined assignments within the specified time frames and according to the expectations given, I will consider additional measures to address continued performance concerns, which may include recommending termination of your employment. Please let me know if you have any questions or concerns.

I have read and understand this PIP, and I have had the opportunity to discuss it with my supervisor. I understand that termination is a possible consequence if I do not meet and sustain the expectations contained in this PIP.

Employee's Signature   Date

cc: Reviewing Manager
       Human Resources

Here are two additional ways to format Performance Improvement Plans:

To: **Employee and File**

Subject: **Performance Improvement Plan**

On (*date*) we met to discuss your performance. During this meeting, I informed you that your performance rating for the annual review period (*date*) to (*date*) was "Below Standards." As indicated in your year-end performance evaluation, you required improvement in budget analyses, interpersonal relationships and timely work flow, all of which are important components/performance factors in your work as Deputy Director of Strategic Planning for our trade association.

In order to help you improve your performance in the areas noted above, I developed the following Performance Improvement Plan (PIP). Your performance improvement period will begin on (*date*) and end on (*date*). I would like you to schedule an hour with me every two weeks to discuss your progress toward the milestones listed below. I would also like you to document your progress in writing so we can use this information as talking points at our bi-monthly meetings.

An "Achieved Standards" level of performance will include the satisfactory accomplishment and demonstration of the following performance factors:

Job Knowledge

Performance Concern

You have been employed in the department for 16 months and have not consistently demonstrated sufficient understanding of the basics of budgetary analyses, a major responsibility outlined in your job description. You continued to make the same errors on (*date, date, and date*). You received training and did not ask for follow-up training or assistance.

You demonstrated problems interpreting data submitted by three of the six departments for which you have strategic planning responsibilities on (*date, date, and date*).

Performance Expectations

- Complete a basic budget analyses course within one month; demonstrate ability to understand and integrate next round of budget submissions within two months following the completion of the course.

- Propose a more detailed development plan for yourself within five weeks, including training in conceptual development of financial plans and basic statistical analysis.

Interpersonal Relationships

Performance Concern

Failure to maintain good interpersonal working relationships with department directors and their staff negatively affects team morale. I have seen you react negatively to co-workers by not being clear about the information you need, not seeking explanations despite continuing concerns about misinterpreted data, avoiding director requests to meet with you, and assigning blame to others for late and erroneous reports. Working on your interpersonal skills will enable you to work more favorably and efficiently with your colleagues.

An example of this occurred on (*date*) when, despite three requests from the Education Director seeking clarity about data you requested from her, you submitted an analysis that incompletely reflected two of her major initiatives.

Performance Expectations

- Be available to others.
- Listen to your colleagues' concerns and respond promptly, checking to make sure you're all on one track.
- Take ownership of your errors.
- Include training in teamwork in the development plan due in five weeks. Human Resources can assist in identifying this training, which should be completed within three months.
- More positive interpersonal relationships should begin immediately and be sustained.

Quantity of Work

Performance Concern

Due to constant revisions because of incomplete and incorrect analyses, the lag in work flow is impeding the critical task of targeting department goals and budgets for the next fiscal year. This has resulted in a general lack of confidence about our association's capability to provide the board of directors with a new fiscal year strategic plan by the annual meeting. For example, last month's submission linking education and constituent outreach did not factor in legislative support. Because you needed to rework the plan, it was submitted late.

Performance Expectation

- During this performance improvement plan period, I will be monitoring the timeliness of your work flow to check that you and the directors are reaching common ground on deadlines and understanding of required input. It is my expectation that you will complete your assignments thoroughly and within deadline.

- Submit draft plans to directors to ensure that they are complete and error-free before finalizing strategic plans.

I will be available to help you throughout this period and beyond. However, you should be aware that if you do not improve your performance to an "Achieved Standards" level by (date), or if you have not completed the previously mentioned assignments within the time frames and expectations given, your employment will be terminated.

However, I look forward to your improved performance and believe it can be sustained. Given an improved performance, there will again be reviews at mid-year and year-end. I believe you can be successful and hope to continue working with you.

Please read this document carefully and make sure that you understand it. If you do not, I will be happy to clarify any point(s).

Signing below will indicate that you have had the opportunity to discuss this Performance Improvement Plan with me and/or a representative from Human Resources. It also indicates your understanding that termination is a possible consequence if you do not meet and sustain the expectations contained in this Performance Improvement Plan.

Signature   Date

Greg Galaida, Employee Relations and Recruitment Manager at the Council on Foundations, believes the key to any good performance improvement plan form is adaptability. "There are just so many factors to be considered—role of the position within the organization, timing of the production cycle, tenure with the company, labor contracts or agreements, the organization's investment in training the individual, possible legal issues, department morale, and external factors affecting performance, just to name a few—that to be wed to a single approach can only mean problems down the line. The Council's form is intentionally skeletal so the necessary meat can be added on a case-by-case basis."

Galaida emphasized that "certainly equity and fairness issues must be considerations as well. Has the employee received adequate guidance and time to perform his or her duties? Is a particular class of employee being singled out by the supervisor? Does the supervisor have a history of a 'hair trigger' approach to management? A positive answer to any of these can be enough to make an HR professional question the need for an improvement plan."

COUNCIL ON FOUNDATIONS*

PERFORMANCE IMPROVEMENT PLAN

Name _____   Date of Discussion _____

Department _____   Supervisor _____

Instructions: Plans for improvement are critical whenever an employee's performance is rated as **"does not meet requirements."** The supervisor and employee are to jointly complete this form during the evaluation meeting. Identify specific work assignments, required actions, or training designed to support performance improvement in the areas listed below. The employee's progress in the areas identified here will be used to support the employee's next appraisal. Attach additional pages, if needed.

PERFORMANCE FACTORS	ACTION PLAN	STATUS
1.		Review Date: / /
2.		Review Date: / /

143

Performance Improvement Plan p. 2

PERFORMANCE FACTORS	ACTION PLAN	STATUS
3.		Review Date: / /
4.		Review Date: / /

Employee _____ Date _____

Supervisor _____ Date _____

* Reprinted by permission of the Council on Foundations.

Keep It Legal!
By Diane Gold

Fiction is obliged to stick to possibilities. Truth isn't.
—Mark Twain, American icon, steamboat pilot,
and author of *The Adventures of Tom Sawyer*
and *Adventures of Huckleberry Finn.*

In a legal battle, even emerging as the winner may feel like a half-hearted victory. So much time, money, and emotion may be invested that just concluding the case can feel like a win. Prepare performance appraisals carefully and you'll sharply reduce the risks.

Performance appraisals can be challenged on their own, or used as evidence in legal battles tied to other types of employment decisions. The appraisal itself might be challenged if an employee believes it contains language detrimental to his or her career, reputation, job security, or salary increases. It can be challenged if discriminatory language seems to indicate unfair bias. If an employee is part of a "protected" class, being age 40 or older for example, and an appraisal reads, "Carl needs to show more energy," that remark might be construed as an age-related criticism.

When another employment decision is the issue, such as an employee's alleged failure to be promoted, the employee might point to outstanding ratings to show that he or she should have been promoted. If alleging a discriminatory termination, an employee may likewise point to positive appraisals to show value to an employer. Alternatively, an employer can use appraisals to defend a negative employment decision, such as a termination, demotion, disciplinary action, or undesired transfer.

Stay Away From Challenges

To protect against lawsuits, ratings must be fair, consistent, and based on fair and objective criteria. If lawsuits alleging discriminatory appraisals are to be avoided, consistency between performance objectives and the rating itself is vital. If, for example, the appraisal doesn't match job objectives, and the employee is rated on elements that were not clearly articulated, the possibility increases that an employee will yell foul play and allege that the rating is unfair. The employee may question why the rating is "unfair" and, if there is no clear basis for it, the employee may assume the rating is lower and/or negative due to race, religion, sex, national origin, etc.

As long as rating elements are objective and not subjective, a manager will have an easier time defending a rating that has been challenged. If an employee is rated on "friendliness," what does that really mean? What is friendly to one person might be excessive to another. Rating anyone on that criterion is inherently subjective and difficult to measure. Examples of more objective evaluations include measuring how many closings a salesperson has made, how often a copywriter has met editorial deadlines, or whether a vice president has brought projects in on budget 90 percent of the time. While it's not always possible to quantify rating elements in numbers, aiming for objectivity makes it easier for managers to prepare ratings and easier for employees to understand them. It may also keep you out of court.

Without measurable criteria, defending a rating can get tricky. Subjective criteria, such as attitude, personality, demeanor, and enthusiasm, can lead to discrimination suits because employees might have a harder time understanding what the supervisor wanted. Additionally, the employee will be more likely to believe he or she is being rated unfairly, misjudged, or discriminated against. While it's not always easy to be 100 percent objective in measuring every employee, seeking objectivity as a clear standard will limit the possibility of legal trouble.

It's also vital that supervisors keep a running file of notes on their employees' performance. This ensures a contemporaneous performance record with specific examples to cite. With careful records in hand, supervisors won't have to dig into their memories. It's also more likely that they will produce an appraisal that fairly reflects the whole appraisal period, not just recent events. Having this documentation becomes critical if the rating is ever challenged.

EEO Compliance

Staying out of legal trouble means rating employees equitably, based on their skills and abilities. With performance ratings, as well as all other employment decisions, it is against federal law to consider an employee's race, color, age, sex, religion, national origin, pregnancy, or disability when evaluating performance. These are the federally protected groups. There are often state, county and/or city laws, local rules or ordinances that must be followed. There is no substitute for effective training about the law. When it comes to the law, there is no such thing as second best! In developing appraisals, it's critical to consider only appropriate factors, such as skills and specific examples of performance. The most legally damaging comments in an appraisal blatantly indicate that the rater has considered an employee's race, sex, religion, etc. *The focus must be on performance only.*

Likewise, no factor should be construed as favoritism. Favoritism occurs when employees are rated more positively simply because a supervisor likes them, shares a personal friendship with them, or is attracted to them. Legal troubles can similarly be triggered by ratings that factor in personality conflicts with employees being evaluated. How much an employee is liked or disliked does not belong in the appraisal process. Factoring such feelings into the process is a legal slippery slope. Supervisors may like employees who are similar to themselves. They may feel more comfortable around them and better able to relate to them. But these feelings must be kept in check to prevent claims of bias down the road.

The High Cost of Inflation

Sometimes discrimination suits are brought specifically as a result of a challenged rating. At other times, different employment issues are the crux of the matter and performance ratings are used as evidence of unfair treatment or lack of rater credibility.

When termination is the primary issue, courts may rely on the lack of a negative written performance rating or other written documentation to cast doubt on an employer's defense to the challenged termination. In the case of a plaintiff arguing under the Age Discrimination in Employment Act, the 1967 Federal law prohibiting age-based job discrimination for those 40 and over, the court reasoned that the employer's defense that the plaintiff was a poor performer was not substantiated by written ratings. The court ultimately concluded that using poor job performance, as a reason for his RIF, was "an afterthought[1]."

Positive performance appraisals are often used by plaintiffs in employment cases to show that they are worthy employees who do not deserve undesirable treatment. An employee questioning a demotion or low monetary award will undoubtedly use positive performance ratings to prove that negative action is unfair and unwarranted. Here, again, the bottom line is to focus solely on performance. Documentation of specific examples of performance is essential to support solid ratings. Managers can get into trouble if they inflate ratings, then find that their hands are tied when it's time to let someone go. In a case of discriminatory termination, employees challenging the termination who have a history of positive ratings can be expected to use these ratings as evidence that they are now being treated unfairly.

What the Courts Say

In analyzing discrimination cases, including cases involving performance appraisals, courts follow legal analyses and case law that has been developed pursuant to Title VII of the Civil Rights Act of 1964. Three basic steps are required to prove a case of discrimination. First, the employee is required to prove a *prima facie* case that is considered to raise an inference of discrimination. Second, the employer must come forward with a reason for taking the action in question. Third, in order to prevail on his or her claim, the employee must establish that the employer's reason is not valid, or is merely a pretext for a discriminatory motive. Following is a closer look at these steps, especially with respect to a case alleging a discriminatory performance rating:

Establishing a *prima facie* case of prohibited discrimination means employees must prove three factors:

1. They are part of a protected class.

2. They have suffered an adverse employment action.

3. They have been treated less favorably than someone who is similarly situated who does not belong to their protected class.

Initially, employees are members of a protected class when they are protected by specific federal, state and/or local laws. Although state and local laws vary,[2] federal law protects individuals from discrimination on the basis of race, color, sex (including pregnancy), religion, national origin, age, and disability.

When Is a Bad Appraisal an "Adverse Action?"

As the second factor of a *prima facie* case, employees must prove that their rating constitutes an "adverse action." Poor performance appraisals, along with other business decisions that might make an employee unhappy, aren't necessarily considered adverse actions. Courts generally look at whether the action at issue is a "tangible employment action" that amounts to "a significant change in employment status, such as hiring, firing, failing to promote, reassignment with significantly different responsibilities, or a decision causing a significant change in benefits."[3] While a lower than expected rating itself may not rise to this level, the negative monetary effect of such a rating, such as a lower bonus, cash award and/or salary, can often be considered an adverse action for the purpose of establishing a *prima facie* case. For instance, in a Washington, D.C. case in which the plaintiff received a bonus of $807 based on a rating of "excellent," instead of the $1,355 bonus that her co-worker received with a rating of "outstanding," the court determined that this difference constituted an adverse action for the purposes of presenting a *prima facie* case of discrimination under Title VII.[4]

To complete their *prima facie* case, employees must show that they were treated less favorably than someone in a similar position who is not of their same protected group. If employees can prove all of the elements of the *prima facie* case, the burden then shifts to employers to defend their decision.

Employers should keep in mind, and employees should be aware, that when articulating a legitimate nondiscriminatory reason, credibility will be given to a performance record that is contemporaneous with actual performance. Likewise, it is important to note that courts will frown upon documentation of poor performance made after the fact. Created after an appraisal, such documentation might actually be viewed as trying to cover up a rating that was not based on appropriate or lawful criteria.

When Is an Inconsistent Rating Discriminatory "Pretext?"

After a *prima facie* case is established, a presumption is raised that the motivation behind the employment action was "prohibited discrimination." (*McDonnell Douglas Corporation v. Green*, 411 U.S. 792 (1973)). At this point the employer has the opportunity to overcome the presumption by articulating a valid reason for taking the action (*Texas Department of Community Affairs v. Burdine*, 450 U.S. 248 (1981)). If the employer gives such a reason, the employee can introduce evidence tending to prove that the employer's reason is not valid and is really pretext, and that the real motivation was the prohibited discrimination as alleged. "Pretext" when discussed in the context of ratings means that the employer is not being truthful and that the actual reason for the negative employment action is either discriminatory or otherwise unlawful or inappropriate.

One way an employee can show pretext is to provide evidence that a rating is inconsistent. Ratings can be inconsistent in two ways. First, a rating can be inconsistent with respect to an individual's performance. Either the rating is better than the performance warranted, and that person might be favored, or the rating is worse than is merited by the performance, and that person is disfavored. Second, a ratings process can be inconsistent when only some employees receive ratings, when employees with similar jobs are being rated on different criteria, and when some employees receive extensive explanatory verbiage on their ratings while others have minimal comments or feedback.

When ratings are inconsistent, there is inequity—and perhaps grounds for legal problems. If a lawsuit is pursued a court may find that "[d]eviation from established policy or practice may be evidence of pretext."[5] Once a court finds that the employers' defense is pretextual, it can infer that the employer is trying to cover up a discriminatory motive. In discrimination cases, courts have ruled that if an employee who suddenly gets a bad rating has a new supervisor, pretext won't be proven by the sole fact that the new supervisor's expectations differ from those of previous supervisors.[6] Courts will also look at substantial changes in an employee's work responsibilities as an explanation for a deviation from a pattern of appraisal that has generally been positive.

For an employee to prevail, he or she has the burden of proving the truth by a "preponderance of the evidence" in the record. A "preponderance of the evidence" is "that degree of relevant evidence which a reasonable mind, considering the record as a whole, might accept as sufficient to support a conclusion that the matter asserted is more likely to be true than not true." *U. S. Postal Service Board of Governors v. Aikens*, 460 U.S. 711 (1983); *Furnco Construction Company v. Waters*, 438 U.S. 567 (1978); *International Brotherhood of Teamsters v. United States*, 431 U.S. 324 (1977)).

Special Considerations

Disability

Sometimes an employer gets into legal trouble as a result of talking with an employee about a bad rating. When employers surmise that a bad rating might be the result of a mental or physical problem, they need to guard against asking questions that could reveal a disability. Any questions relating to employee health can be interpreted as disability discrimination in a courtroom. However, if the employee reveals and/or explains that he or she has a medical issue that requires attention, the supervisor should handle the matter with sensitivity and refer the employee to personnel who are trained to handle these types of issues (that is, counselors, nurses, Human Resources, etc.). The focus for the supervisor should be on the performance deficiency itself, and not on speculation about why.

Retaliation

Retaliation claims arise when employees allege they received a lower appraisal than they would have otherwise received because they filed an EEO complaint or engaged in other activity that is considered to be "protected."[7] Employers need to be particularly careful in fairly rating an employee who has engaged in such activity and should keep in mind that it is generally easier to pursue a successful retaliation claim than to prove the initial claim of discrimination itself.

In order to prove a retaliation claim, employees must prove:

1. They engaged in a protected activity.

2. Their employer was aware of the protected activity.

3. The employer took adverse action against them.

4. There was a causal connection between the protected activity and the adverse action. (*McKenna v. Weinberger*, 729 F.2d 783, 790 (D.C. cir. 1984). Demonstrating that the adverse action followed the protected activity within a short period of time is one method of making this causal connection.

Plaintiffs' attorneys who are claiming unlawful retaliation will scrutinize a rating that is received subsequent to the filing of an EEO complaint. If the rating is lower than in prior years, or the language reflects hostility or a previously absent critical tone, there is often fertile ground for a new EEO complaint based on the rating. After an employee files a discrimination charge, or is otherwise involved in a discrimination case, supervisors must take special care to treat that individual fairly. It might be particularly difficult to focus on fairness when there's a perceived unjust challenge, but supervisors must work to keep any acrimonious feelings in check.

Team Evaluations

Of major importance for supervisors is that all individuals participating in evaluations understand and are trained in the process, as well as EEO laws, documentation, and consistency. Should the appraisal and/or appraisal process ever be challenged, a derogatory or otherwise inappropriate comment by one of several evaluators could be seen to taint the entire process.

E-Mail and Other Documentation

When a performance appraisal is challenged in court, a plaintiff's attorney will be able to access and review a wealth of information, any or all of which could help shape the ultimate determination. The documentation reviewed might include prior performance appraisals, other employees' appraisals, and memos and e-mails concerning performance. It's important to note that e-mails are frequently the evidence of choice in employment discrimination cases because people generally take less care when writing an e-mail than when writing official correspondence on company letterhead. Take heed, or your hard drive may show up in court.

The Bottom-Line

Consistently applied and up-to-date policies and procedures, preventive measures in the form of EEO training, and a general work environment of respect and professionalism go a long way toward limiting claims and reducing liability if a manager's actions are challenged.

■ ■ ■ ■ ■ ■ ■ ■ ■ ■ ■ ■

Test Your Legal IQ

Supervisors

❑ Are the rating factors objective?

❑ Do employees understand what is expected of them?

❑ Are you documenting performance during the entire rating period?

❑ Are you communicating with employees about their performances during the rating period?

❑ Are you spending the same amount of time and attention on each employee's performance?

❑ Have you received training on implementing the performance process?

❑ Have you received basic EEO training?

❑ Is your appraisal free from extraneous comments and personal opinions?

❑ Do you give specific examples on the appraisal to demonstrate employees' strengths and/or weaknesses?

❑ Are you rating performance solely on the bases of skills and abilities?

❑ Are you favoring or disfavoring any employee for reasons unrelated to that employee's performance?

❑ Are employment decisions regarding employees consistent with their ratings?

❑ Do employees have the opportunity to review and respond to appraisal?

❑ Are ratings consistent in process and procedure throughout your organization?

❏ Are ratings given a second look (and signed) by a more senior manager?

❏ Are ratings discussed with employees to make sure they understand any deficiencies?

Employees

❏ Do you update your supervisor on all work?

❏ Do you ask for clarification when you need it?

❏ Do you understand the performance expected of you?

❏ Do you know why you receive the ratings you do? Do they seem fair?

❏ Do you track your own progress?

❏ Do you maintain copies of your work products?

❏ Do you initiate conversations with your supervisor on your performance throughout the year?

❏ Were your goals clear at the beginning of the performance cycle?

❏ Do you take responsibility for your performance?

❏ Do you work at full capacity/try your best?

❏ Do you understand the appraisal process at your organization?

❏ If necessary, what have you done to improve your performance?

❏ Do you have an opportunity to respond to your performance reviews? Do you respond in writing?

❏ If you have conflicting views with your supervisor, do you back up your perspective with specific examples?

❏ Was there enough time allotted for your performance discussion?

❏ Do you receive feedback all year?

❏ Do you have the opportunity to review your appraisals in advance, or at the beginning of the meeting?

❏ Do you receive a copy of your performance appraisal?

❏ If you have concerns, do you share them with the Human Resources department?

■ ■ ■ ■ ■ ■ ■

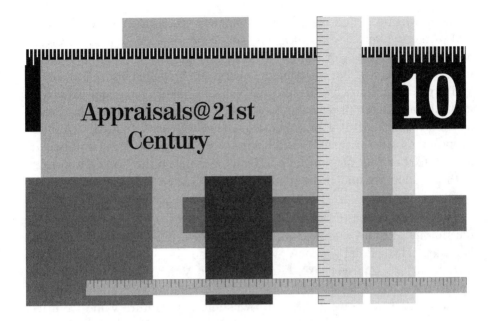

Appraisals@21st Century

10

We shape our tools and then our tools shape us.

—Marshall McLuhan, visionary Canadian educator
who examined the media's significance
as a global gateway.

Dilbert reprinted by permission of United Feature Syndicate, Inc.

We're experiencing what Alvin Toffler might call "an exclamation point in history,"[1] an era in which old barriers fall and there is vast reorganization of the production and distribution of knowledge and the symbols used to communicate it.[2] Toffler wrote about GenCorp Automotive in

Indiana, which opened a $65 million plant in the early 1990s with about 500 workers. Every worker, not only supervisors and managers, received $8,000–$10,000 worth of training—not just in the technical tasks of making car body panels, but in problem solving, leadership skills, role playing, and organization process. Employees work in teams, and every team has multiple tasks so employees can switch jobs and minimize boredom. Team leaders receive a full year's training, including visits abroad.[3] "As the economy moves forward," Toffler wrote, "all firms are being compelled to rethink the role of knowledge...They operate on the assumption that both productivity and profits will skyrocket if...the full potential of the worker is tapped."[4]

GenCorp is committed to reciprocal payback and retention. Given the fluidity of today's work climate, there is also the concept of wetware. Wetware? If you don't yet know, welcome to the 21st century. There's hardware, software, and wetware. Used by Silicon Valley firms, hardware refers to physical assets, software to recipes for creating value, and wetware to employee brainpower.[5] "A firm owns and can capture value from its hardware and software, but it only rents its wetware. Wetware is the private property of individual employees who can take it with them to another firm if they choose. To generate shareholder value, managers must find ways to convert the knowledge contained in employee wetware—even knowledge employees may not realize they have—into software. The firm then owns the software and can use it to create and capture value for its shareholders."[6]

That idea is alive well beyond Silicon Valley. Already employers and periodicals refer to the idea of addressing needs rather than filling jobs. In Washington, D.C., there is discussion about bringing technical consultants in to fill certain government jobs, contracting with them only for the time needed to deliver desired results. Fast changes in today's work climate—flextime, telecommuting, job sharing, and improved training, among a long list of others—make it possible, even feasible, to look at a fresh, fluid approach. A lagging economy and major staff cuts make it a necessity.

Still not easy or even understandable in many traditional work settings, performance appraisals, too, need to adapt to change, especially with a workforce that is getting older—and younger. A decade ago, in private industry, employees ages 55 or older comprised 11.9 percent of the working population. In 2000, that figure jumped to 12.9 percent. By 2010, it's projected to leap to an estimated 16.9 percent.[7] And just as baby boomers made their mark on the business world, 44 million Gen Xers are starting to do the same.

Moving up fast are the Gen-Yers. Born between 1979 and 1994, they're now "entering the workforce in earnest, with a lot of raw energy, unbridled enthusiasm, and the skills and experience of much older workers."[8] Gen-Yers "live to be trained" and "absolutely thrive on recognition."[9]

With matrix management, work groups, team projects, multiple raters, multiple supervisors and more, there is an accelerating team mindset. Just as so many of today's personnel practices, this one isn't new either. Sanford Jacoby reported that, "self-managing work teams were evident in the 1870s, when groups of workers negotiated with owners for tonnage rates for each job, then decided on pay distribution, whom to hire, and how to organize and train for the job."[10] What is new is the prevalence of the team focus. Teamwork is not just a buzzword but a concept that is threading its way through organizational structures. In some cases, as in matrix management, it is changing structures, injecting a zest into organizations that is giving a facelift to business as usual.

■ ■ ■ ■ ■ ■ ■ ■ ■ ■ ■ ■

"Psychological Turnover"

"Retention issues are changing with the market," said Dr. Beverly Kaye at a Society for Human Resource Management forum. Kaye is co-author of *Love 'Em or Lose 'Em: Getting Good People to Stay*. Kaye said that rather than physically walking out the door, staff may "check out" by abandoning motivation and productivity, which creates "psychological turnover." While talented staff may hang around during a sluggish job market, it's going to take more than fear to hold them over the long run.

Kaye said it takes the following to keep talent and boost staff performance:

▣ Recognize there's a serious shortage of talent.

▣ Recognize that the worst of this shortage has yet to hit—it will come by 2008, as boomers retire and there are less younger workers.

▣ Know that employers spend three times as much to recruit as they do to retrain.

▣ Understand that people stay for reasons beyond pay—employers must be competitive on dollars and win on culture.

▣ Understand why staff stay or leave—conduct periodic "stay interviews" not just exit interviews.

- ◙ Make retention everyone's job.
- ◙ Recognize that mentoring is central to retention.
- ◙ Recognize that there will always be a higher bidder.

■ ■ ■ ■ ■ ■ ■

Collaboration...Less an Ideal, More an Expectation

Change is rarely easy. Even the concept of collaboration is still being explored. "The popular culture gives much more credit to individual genius than to collaborative genius," author Michael Schrage told the *Washington Post*'s Don Oldenburg.[12] Published more than a decade ago, Schrage's book, *Shared Minds: The New Technologies of Collaboration* is perhaps more applicable today, when collaboration is less an ideal and more of an expectation. "Being a collaborator doesn't mean giving up who you are," Schrage said. "It means using someone else to amplify you at the same time that the other person is using you to amplify [himself or herself.]...That Laurel wasn't as funny without Hardy speaks only to the success of the collaboration, not to the failure of either individual... Did it take away from Picasso because he collaborated with Braque to create Cubism? No."[13]

Schrage said that while the "need to collaborate is becoming less ambiguous," the tools are still primitive. "We are at the Alexander Graham Bell stage of collaborative tools. Once Graham invented the telephone, you could see where it might lead. Given collaborative technology, given environments that encourage creative interaction, the 'good communication' that has been given so much lip service will seem like a one-night stand compared to the impact collaboration has on the quality of relationships— business and otherwise."[14]

Even given the tools, there must be the will to apply them. Smart companies manage change by embracing it. World Wide Technology's CEO, David Steward, put it this way: "No matter what I've faced, personally or professionally, what keeps me going is a passage from The Life and Letters of Charles Darwin, 'It's not the strongest or the smartest that survive, but the ones most adaptable to change.'"[15] Duke Ellington put it another way: "Life has two rules: Number one, never quit. Number two, always remember number one." [16]

Synygy, Inc. provides performance and other management software to such corporate giants as DuPont and Sun Microsystems. Prizing close teamwork and continuing feedback despite rapid growth, Synygy developed an employee-evaluation program characterized by quarterly reviews. "'The whole idea of having an evaluation is to help you improve your performance,' managing director Anil Chouhan said. 'But if you're going to change behavior, you have to get the information to do it in a timely fashion—this way, you can decide that you need to work on these particular things over the next three months, and quickly see the results." [17]

With 3,400 employees and sales of $157 million, Herman Miller, Inc, an office furniture company, is working to shift appraisals away from merely measuring results. In using the appraisal process as a way to build teamwork among employees and supervisors, "the company emphasizes that management is a function, not a class," serving to cut down on performance appraisal anxiety.[18] The Italian firm, Fiat, combines objective and subjective performance measures into a single, integrated system. Fiat's top 500 managers work under a management by objectives process in which they have performance indicators tied to profit and debt objectives, customer service, and increasing sales in a particular market, among several other indicators. Meeting objectives earns them up to 30 percent of base salary—*if* the larger group meets its objectives, too. The Fiat Group, for example, has 16 sectors, each headed by a manager. Six managers might meet all of their performance goals. But if the other 10 managers don't, none of the managers receive a bonus.[19] The incentive for teamwork is strong and measurable.

■ ■ ■ ■ ■ ■ ■ ■ ■ ■ ■ ■

Managing Change[20]

◨ Know the current situation.

◨ Develop a clear picture of where the organization needs to go.

◨ Set specific goals and dates by which to achieve that vision.

◨ Outline the transition state in detail.

◨ Determine what needs to be done to achieve the desired change. The organization's subsystems of people, structure, technology, and tasks need to be directed to be compatible with the change.

◨ Develop and execute the plan for managing the transition state.

■ ■ ■ ■ ■ ■ ■

■ ■ ■ ■ ■ ■ ■ ■ ■ ■ ■

Jump-Starting Results[21]

In the Harvard Business Review on Change, Robert H. Schaffer and Harvey A. Thomson state, "There is no reason for senior-level managers to acquiesce when their people plead they are already accomplishing just about all that can be accomplished, or that factors beyond their control are blocking accelerated performance improvement...Instead management needs to recognize there is an abundance of both unexploited capability and dissipated resources in the organization."

Here's how they suggest driving new opportunities—and jump-starting good results:

◘ **Ask each unit to set and achieve a few ambitious short-term performance goals.** Every organization can improve with resources at hand. There might be faster turnaround time on customer requests, test of a managerial process, or cost-savings.

◘ **Periodically review progress, capture the essential learning, and reformulate strategy.** Learn what is and isn't actually working. Fresh insights can generate new support, changed methods, and the confidence that comes from overhauling obsolete practices.

◘ **Institute the changes that work—and discard the rest.** Integrate the practices and technologies that contribute most to performance improvement.

◘ **Create the context and identify the crucial business challenges.** Establish a broader, strategic framework to guide continuing improvement.

■ ■ ■ ■ ■ ■ ■

Making Convictions Operational

Adapting performance appraisals, even developing and implementing them effectively to begin with, never occurs in a vacuum. The broader work climate must embrace those needs. And the will to do that begins at the top—possibly after some convincing stops on the way up. But once a CEO is philosophically committed to putting those assets that don't go home at night first, it's up to management to turn this conviction into operational fact. That requires communication, more communication, training, and monitoring and assessment. It takes, as Toffler framed it, "thinking about 'big things' while you're doing 'small things,' so that all the small things go in the right direction."[22] Championing the big things, such as organizational vision, takes many routes, all of which can help shape a positive performance appraisal process.

Communication

Leaders talk about leadership, usually enthusiastically. Microsoft chair Bill Gates said, "What I do best is spread my enthusiasm."[23] Microsoft CEO Steve Ballmer said, "The end point must be exciting enough to stir thousands to uncommon effort."[24] Chairman, Herb Kelleher, explained that Southwest Airlines gives employees the "opportunity to be a maverick. You don't have to fit into a constraining mold—you can have a good time."[25] Asked by a *BusinessWeek* columnist to sum up why he had been so successful at GE, former CEO Jack Walsh said, "My main job was developing talent. I was a gardener providing water and nourishment."[26]

Still a survey conducted jointly by the Society for Human Resource Management and Personnel Decisions International found that 22 percent of participants said the greatest challenge they face is a lack of support from top management. Forty-two percent of the organizations that took part reported that executives do not even bother to review the performance management systems currently in place.[27]

As underscored throughout this book, almost everything an organization does tells its employees how much they count. For employees to feel valued, they must be valued. Expecting them to be on board with the organizational mission means they must genuinely be a part of that mission, and clear about how. The vision focus of Chapter 4 needs to dovetail with the recognition content of Chapter 5. A performance appraisal that recaps continuing dialogue says the employee is vital to moving the vision. A perfunctory annual review says the opposite.

Organizations invite two-way communications in innumerable ways—from daily e-mail Qs and As, chat rooms, and town hall meetings, to Friday pizza parties, more formal meetings, and sit-downs with the CEO. Some companies conduct anonymous surveys, asking such questions as, "What's the best thing about working here?" "What three things would you change?" "What makes you proud to be here? "In Sydney, Australia, an employee was chosen by lottery and asked "What would you do if you were CEO for a day?"[28] A CEO might tell some tales about his or her own appraisals.

Welcoming employees to articulate values can be especially helpful in advance of a corporate restructuring, or in planning a product launch, design of new symbols, or perhaps redesign of the appraisal process. Management consultants and authors James C. Collins and Jerry I. Porras often recommend "a Mars Group," a diverse group of employees they call "a representative slice of the company's genetic code."[29] A Mars Group works like this:

> "Imagine that you've been asked to recreate the very best attributes of your organization on another planet but you have seats on the rocket ship for only five to seven people. Whom should you send? Most likely, you'll choose the people who have a gut level understanding of your core values, the highest level of credibility with their peers, and the highest level of competence. We'll often ask people brought together to work on core values to nominate a Mars Group of five to seven people (not necessarily from the assembled group). Invariably they end up selecting highly credible representatives who do a super job of articulating the core values precisely because they are exemplars of those values—a representative slice of the company's genetic code."[30]

More than 2,000 years ago, Aristotle observed that, "If communication is to change behavior, it must be grounded in the desires and interests of the receivers. Since 350 B.C., there have been no major changes in that central idea. To be noticed, communications must contain something that interests the receivers; to change behavior, it must touch one of their values."[31]

■ ■ ■ ■ ■ ■ ■ ■ ■ ■ ■ ■

Embracing Talent[32]

▣ Make talent management a critical part of every manager's job.

▣ Create a winning "employee value proposition" that provides a compelling reason for a highly talented person to join and stay with your company.

▣ Rebuild your recruiting strategies to inject talent at all levels, and from many sources, to respond to the ebbs and flows in the talent market.

▣ Weave development into the organization by deliberately using stretch jobs, candid feedback, coaching, and mentoring to grow every manager's talents.

■ Differentiate the performance of your people, and affirm their unique contributions to the organization.

■ ■ ■ ■ ■ ■ ■

Training

Touching employee values means that, just as setting work objectives and conducting appraisals, the training needs to be in line with what will actually work. How much will the training count on an everyday basis? Are there supports in place to leverage the training? How will related growth and development be fostered once the power point presentation goes dark?

In *The Fifth Discipline*, Peter Senge wrote that "organizations learn only through individuals who learn."[33] Yet many organizations offer little or no training when it comes to evaluating performance and conducting performance appraisal interviews. It often seems that firms believe promotion to a supervisory or management position automatically gives an individual the ability to perform all managerial functions without the benefit of formalized training. Most performance appraisal problems could be eliminated through proper training, training that begins with promotion to a supervisor position, and training that is reinforced through at least annual updating sessions.[34]

Basic to any appraisal training are techniques to apply work standards and set them jointly with employees. Rating errors should also be high on the list. Coaching and counseling skills based on directly observed behavior are also essential to a solid training agenda. "'Management by Wandering Around a concept popularized by Tom Peters, ...is the tactic of observing what's occurring firsthand, and it's a good one. Mishandled— and it's easy to do—it often becomes 'management by stumbling around.'"[35] Training in the performance system should be directed to both employees and managers. And it should be designed based on how adults learn. Deborah Lamber of the Utah Chapter of the National Society of Performance and Instruction wrote that adults will learn only what they feel a need to learn, will seek to learn what they have identified as important, look to learning what can be immediately applied, and learn by doing.[36] Employees trained in performance appraisals become empowered to take charge of their own performance. They are better prepared to initiate discussions about their work and to do self-appraisals on a continuing basis. After participating in training, employees should be able to understand the process, monitor their own performance, be clear about the importance of taking responsibility for their work, accept feedback and pursue their own professional development. They should benefit from understanding the importance of performance management in their organization and their particular role in bolstering it.

Retraining should occur each year. Be sure new employees and managers are introduced to the performance system early on. Don't forget managers promoted from within. Training is especially key when a new system is introduced. Benchmark and stay abreast of best practices, tracking what's working at other organizations.

To receive consistent feedback is perhaps the biggest pay-off for the employee. Employees deserve to know where their talents are and how they can build more skills and develop professionally. Richard Franklin, a human resources manager at KnowledgePoint, says, "Surveys have shown that employees will stay with a company because they felt they were getting feedback. They want to know how they are doing and how they can improve."[37]

■ ■ ■ ■ ■ ■ ■ ■ ■ ■ ■ ■ ■

For Sound Appraisals...[38]

1. Understand rating errors.

2. Understand how to process observed information.

3. Understand how to establish a frame of reference for what is observed.

4. Be familiar with the performance appraisal system in use.

5. Experience observing a performance appraisal.

6. Practice effective interviewing techniques.

7. Practice conducting a performance appraisal.

■ ■ ■ ■ ■ ■ ■ ■

Monitoring and Assessment

"As constant change becomes a way of life in organizations, the job skill with the biggest pay-off is the ability to learn—and unlearn, and relearn, " said John H. Zenger, chairman of the Times Mirror Group.[39]

The operational word here is learn. Despite the best efforts, communicating and training are not necessarily change agents. Just because they occur does not mean they are working. Or if they are working, it may be short-lived. Is the pay-off immediate? Still going strong in a month? Six months? Is there really fresh understanding? And if so, is it being demonstrated in new, desired ways, or is performance basically unchanged?

The process is eased by quality hiring, in which a "good fit" upfront translates into eager, dedicated employee performance on most days. But given that the communication and training are meant for current employees, the aim is to make them work well and leverage the benefits as widely as possible. With performance appraisals, it's easier to gauge the effects than with some other initiatives designed for behavior change. Are supervisors making less rating errors? Are employees more engaged? Is talk about setting objectives livelier and maybe a genuine debate? Are mini-reviews occurring more frequently, or perhaps for the first time? There's observable behavior plus the "gut barometer" to draw on—and it's important to stay tuned. Investing in communications and training will be counterproductive if performance remains unchanged.

Feedback should be sought soon after the training or specific communications, and again at a later time. "In the study of human behavior psychologists discovered a long time ago that feedback is one of the most critical requirements for sustained high-level performance of any human act. Without frequent and specific feedback, performance varies and often fails."[40] "It has been estimated that approximately 50 percent of the nonperformance problems in business occur because of lack of feedback."[41] Even after receiving sound training or communications, workers need feedback about how they are demonstrating its effects.

When NCCI Holdings, Inc., a Boca Raton-based nonprofit consortium that provides data on workplace injury claims to insurance companies, began receiving customer complaints about spotty service and noticed growing demoralization of employees after fighting off a takeover in the late 1990s, NCCI's management decided to take a hard look at the way it managed human capital. The HR department spent a year studying the problem and, in 1999, NCCI unrolled an employee evaluation system that evaluates employees not once but twice a year. This new system gave employees two chances each year to have an impact on their compensation and it gave management that ability to set highly specific objectives for employees to meet. It also worked continuously to improve performance with a coaching system that was closely linked to the evaluation process. The system is quite rigorous to implement, requiring an extensive schedule of meetings throughout the year, including 360-degree feedback, supervisors' roundtables, and individualized coaching sessions with employees. Two years after the new system was implemented, turnover and customer complaints were down.[42] Monitoring and measuring the outcome showed a clear link to objectives set for employees and customers.

21st Century Challenges

We introduced this chapter with "wetware," the brainpower that organizations are dedicated to converting to value. A look at McDonald's Corporation traces how this occurs. When the first McDonald's began feeding us in 1956, the company's hardware consisted of property and equipment. Its most valued asset was software, with its revolutionary formula for McDonald's products. This formula helped build golden arches all over the world. Despite fast accelerating competition, McDonald's persisted and remained strong. Enter the Filet-O-Fish sandwich, and an excellent example of how wetware is converted to software. At first, McDonald's sold just hamburgers and fries, a limited line designed for speed and efficiency. But one franchisee, in a predominantly Catholic area, couldn't sell meat on Fridays and developed a fish sandwich. Fearing the innovation would lead to inconsistency across franchise units, McDonald's resisted initially, then captured the wetware and turned it into software that's put Filet-O-Fish on the map. The Big Mac came into being in much the same way. It was the brainchild of a franchisee in Pittsburgh who wanted a heftier sandwich to satisfy steelworkers.[43]

"The demands on the skill, knowledge, performance, responsibility, and integrity of the manager have doubled in every generation during the past half century,"[44] and the current one is no exception. In a competitive, urgent, and shrinking world, converting wetware into value is a hot commodity. Envisioning how 21st century businesses will be "seen, understood and managed entirely as an integrated process," Peter Drucker wrote that "manager[s] will have to acquire a whole new set of tools—many of which [they] will have to develop themselves. [They] will need to acquire adequate yardsticks for performance and results in the key areas of business objectives...[They] will have to acquire the new tools of the decision-making process.[45] Drucker also pointed out that "the best and most dedicated people are ultimately volunteers."[46] Indicating that as companies move into the 21st century they will need to draw on the full creative energy and talent of their people, Collins and Porras asked: "Why people should give full measure?" Drawing on the "Mars Group" noted previously, they conceived of asking each member, "How could we frame the purpose of this organization so that if you woke up each morning with enough money to retire, you would nevertheless keep working here? What deeper sense of purpose would motivate you to continue to dedicate your precious creative energies to this company's efforts?"[47]

What they're suggesting is a "core ideology that is meaningful and in-spirational to people inside the organization; it need not be exciting to outsiders...A clear, well-articulated ideology attracts to the company people whose core values are compatible with those of the company; conversely it repels those whose personal values are incompatible...Nike, for instance, has a campus that seems more like a shrine to the competitive spirit than a corporate office."[48] Collins and Porras carefully differentiate between core ideology and core competence. "Core competence is a strategic concept that defines an organization's capabilities—what it's particularly good at. Core ideology captures what you stand for and why you exist."[49]

Four Seasons Hotel and Resorts' performance management philosophy makes clear not only that the performance appraisal is provided to build effective supervisor/employee relationships but that there "should be a uniformity of performance format, administration and rating criteria throughout all hotels." Four Season hotels are global, and the performance appraisal is an active tool in ensuring that the standards are, too.

Globalization presents particular 21st century challenges. One survey of senior executives indicated that of 60 issues identified, 12 were HR problems.[50] Two of the four top concerns were "company-wide loyalty and motivation" and "appraising performance."

Add a queasy economy with RIFs to the mix, and appraisals become even more vital. Conducted effectively, they are essential in clarifying organizational expectations, rewarding good performance, recognizing specific employee interests, and providing a predictable structure in an often tough, uncertain world. Twenty-first century opportunities do present some new challenges. Here are suggested approaches to handling them:

Flextime

Because companies define flextime differently, it can be difficult to translate best practices from one organization to another. Many different arrangements are made to help employees maintain more balanced lives. For some companies, flextime is identified as a core time when all employees are expected to be at the office or work location. With advance notice, other employers allow major adjustments in the weekly schedule. Another model compresses hours into a shortened workweek.

The Bureau of Labor Statistics reported that, in May 2001, about 28.8 percent, or 29 million full-time wage and salary workers used flextime, a number that has almost doubled over the past decade.[51] A study by William M. Mercer of 800 firms with 1,000 or more employees found that 34 percent use compressed work weeks for some part of their workforce and an additional 14 percent are considering this approach.[52]

Flextime appears to contribute to decreased tardiness, reduced absenteeism, less job fatigue, increased organizational loyalty, and improved recruitment.[53] At Baxter International, a global medical products and services firm, nearly 20 percent of employees take advantage of some form of alternative work schedule. Griffin Lewis, vice president of logistics, says that the program pays off in boosted morale, more effective recruiting, better stress management, and increased productivity.[54]

The performance management process should not be adversely affected. Objectives should be set and measured at regularly scheduled mini-reviews. The employee must show a willingness to do quality work and make the new schedule predictable and seamless. To minimize problems, employees should stay organized and leave detailed directions for the supervisor and coworkers. Both supervisor and employee should be accessible when the unexpected occurs. They need to work at keeping each other in the loop. Because flextime often needs time to work, a pilot time frame can be agreed to upfront, and an evaluation discussion scheduled. As needed, flextime can be adjusted or discontinued.

■■■■■■■■■■■■

Flextime Works[55]

▣ Short-term absences are reduced because of greater control over schedules.

▣ Tardiness is reduced because the workday begins when the employee arrives.

▣ Morning coffee breaks are reduced due to staggered hours.

▣ Employees are more likely to work during their most productive hours: mornings for early birds, evenings for night owls.

▣ Workers are more focused on doing the job as opposed to spending time in the office.

▣ Business can offer more flexible service to customers.

▣ Supervisors are forced to communicate more effectively because employees are not always in the office.

■ ■ ■ ■ ■ ■ ■

Telecommuting

Telecommuting is here to stay. Whether an issue of space, employee retention, or just linking work and home, it's usually a hit. A survey of 754 human resources professionals, conducted in 2001 by the Society for Human Resource Management, showed a steady climb from 20 percent of employers offering telecommuting in 1997 to 37 percent in 2001. According to an International Telework Advisory Council 2001 survey, there were 28 million Americans teleworking. Other Council studies indicate that teleworkers have an average of 10 percent higher employee satisfaction and 10 to 30 percent higher productivity. Employee retention has climbed as much as 22 percent.

The Council identifies four success factors for a Telework Program: dedicated resources; automated processes and technology; job function considerations; and manager characteristics. The manager should have above average organizational, planning, and coaching skills; be able to focus on output rather than hours; be able to establish and evaluate well-defined measurable objectives and goals; and provide timely and constructive feedback.[56] Managers should also be comfortable managing employees who are not in their "line of vision." Employees should be reliable, disciplined, and able to get work done with limited supervision. Good time management and communication skills really matter.

At Merrill Lynch, the company developed a manager's guide and provided training sessions. At a major association in Washington, DC, a staff person is designated as a liaison between the supervisor and the employee to ensure that discussions around expectations and deliverables take place. "Task scheduling, meeting scheduling, and visit frequency should be spelled out clearly so that the employee knows how much contact is expected with the office. Having measures and guidelines can become especially important for jobs where the teleworker's output is not effectively measurable. It is crucial to note that the guidelines should be loose enough to allow the telecommuter some flexibility. It is important to establish boundaries; however, they should not be so strict that they hinder the performance of the employee."[57]

Telework consultant Yvonne Zhou, president of Futrend Technology Inc. in Virginia, says, "A teleworker must be evaluated as a nonteleworker. Telework forces managers to measure by performance, not by face time or the number of hours an employee is in the office."

Training managers and employees is critical to ensure performance and high productivity among teleworkers and the success of a telework program. Managers need to learn how to manage, motivate, and collaborate with their teleworking staff. Managers must be shown how to develop clear performance standards and measures that evaluate an employee's performance based on objective criteria. The expectations must be discussed upfront. Employees should be self-disciplined and able to handle varying situations. The supervisor and employee should agree to review the arrangement frequently and make changes or discontinue as needed.

Job-Sharing

"There is a strong business case for job-sharing," says Honey Melville-Brown, a consultant who helped compile a study showing that "Not only in terms of performance, but also as a critical retention tool, job sharing is an excellent way to fill the skills gap. It may be a company's ideal to have a single, full-time person, but [companies] are realizing that it's better to have the right skills package spread across two bodies than an inadequate one in one."[58]

The challenge is to distribute tasks fairly and build strong communication between the job-sharers so that coworkers and customers aren't affected. Here, too, strong, measurable standards, consistent monitoring of performance, and continuing, clear communication are key.

Performance evaluation in job-sharing is similar to evaluating part-time workers. Goal-setting is a major element. Responsibilities can be divided in ways that make sense and promote work continuity. If each worker is clear on the objectives that he or she is responsible for, it ensures the accountability needed.

Team Performance Appraisals

Two assessments are needed here—for team performance and individual performance. Understanding and reinforcing the balance is important to the success of both, especially in organizations that value and promote teamwork. It takes motivated individuals to spur on the team. Many organizations now factor behaviors beneficial to team development into their criteria for individual performance. Employees are expected to deliver results in specific ways.

"In a case study of self-managed groups at the Digital Equipment Corporation in Colorado Springs, Carol Norman and Robert Zwacki found that team appraisal appeared to improve participation, commitment, and productivity. The need to participate is reinforced by the requirement for all team members to take specific roles and responsibilities for performance appraisals."[59]

Yet despite becoming a sacred cow to American businesses, a Mercer Management study found that just 13 of 179 teams received high ratings. "Somehow we need to get past this idea that all we have to do is join hands and sing Kumbaya and say, 'We've moved to teamwork.' Many companies are narrowing the focus and horizon of teams."[60]

■ ■ ■ ■ ■ ■ ■ ■ ■ ■ ■ ■

Why Teams Fail[61]

- ▣ **Mental Opt-Out**. Busy managers surrender without any real effort. Fully half the decisions reached by teams are never implemented.

- ▣ **Dueling Advice**. At first, everyone is very polite. The teams storm. Months pass before things settle down.

- ▣ **Old-fashioned Pay Schemes**. Companies move on to teams but keep their old individual performance measures. Team-based pay for rewarding the entire team for meeting goals is not in place.

■ ■ ■ ■ ■ ■ ■

Virtual teams bring benefits along with complications. Just as with telecommuting, the supervisor's reliance on line-of-sight managing can bring discomfort to this work arrangement.

Carl Worthy, an expert on remote workers, explained, "Managers are process-focused. They think, 'I know you're doing a good job because I see you working.' Because that's impossible with virtual teams, managers have to focus on results. Managers also may find it difficult to coach and advise, assess training needs, and give feedback to team members who aren't in view. Reviews using 360-degree feedback can help managers understand how members are performing, and analyzing bulletin boards and intranets will give a feel for the team's issues and problems."[62]

Matrix Management

With appraisal issues similar to those of team evaluations, matrix management involves both horizontal and vertical reporting. Two or more intersecting lines of authority can run through the same individual, who typically reports to two supervisors. A scientist, for example, may be working in a line office on ocean and coastal issues. Because a coral reef matrix team is set up, and there's a clear link between ocean and coastal health and survival of coral reefs, he or she joins that team, too, reporting to both the line office supervisor and the head of the new matrix team. Other line office scientists, focused on weather, habitat, and other linked areas will join the matrix team as well. Matrix management considerably leverages knowledge and skills, and opens opportunities for employees to branch out from their usual offices and disciplines and generate a stronger, better-informed end product.

In 1992, Intel Corporation created a matrix organization by staffing five major product groups, such as multimedia and supercomputing components, with people from basic functional groups, such as finance, marketing, business development, and software technology. Individual Intel employees became members of both product and functional groups.[63]

In matrix structures, the main or functional manager typically has primary responsibility for performance reviews, with matrix team leaders or product managers providing input.

Multiple Rater Appraisals and Multiple Supervisors

Various situations arise when there are multiple raters. For fairness and employee comfort, it is extremely important to be sure all on board are thoroughly grounded in what is being measured and whom is being evaluated—the employee should not feel as if this is a town meeting. Everyone's role should be clear—and to the employee as well.

Just as in matrix management, it is usually the primary supervisor who takes the lead, with input from one or more supervisors who share management responsibility.

Goal setting is crucial. All supervisors must agree on goals and the value or weight assigned to each goal. This establishes the priorities that will guide employee performance throughout the evaluation cycle. All supervisors should also commit to being available as needed to offer support and direction. Periodic mini-reviews are key to keeping everyone on the same track.

Upward Performance Appraisals

Mention employees appraising managers and managers often cringe. In part, upward appraisals are an extension of customer-focused thinking—those on the receiving end are the best ones to evaluate it. Today's employees also don't want to be cogs. They seek knowledge and understanding about their worlds and want to put that information to good use. Two-way evaluations often appeal to them.

Several challenges face an employer willing to give upward appraisals a shot. Should the employee/evaluators be anonymous? Anonymous appraisals are more likely to result in honest feedback. And how should the appraisal be designed so it doesn't just sink into a popularity contest? The employee also needs to really know his or her supervisor's work firsthand—no long distance speculation.

While research has shown that supervisors did improve performance as a result of anonymous upward appraisals, it not surprisingly also shows that supervisors who receive upward appraisals view feedback more positively than when the feedback is not anonymous. Conversely, employees view the process more positively when it is anonymous.[64] Managers who received the appraisal and subsequent coaching are frequently the biggest supporters of the upward appraisal process.

This process requires employees to evaluate their supervisors on a set of preestablished criteria, often having to do with supervisory style and effectiveness. Any employer who wants to implement upward appraisals must be sure that evaluation criteria are unmistakably clear. It's best to pilot the process before there's an official launch.

■ ■ ■ ■ ■ ■ ■ ■ ■ ■ ■ ■

Sample Upward Appraisal[65]

For each of the following statements, rate your supervisor on a scale of 1 to 5.

> 1 = Never does this.
>
> 2 = Does this sometimes.
>
> 3 = Does this about half the time.
>
> 4 = Does this most of the time.
>
> 5 = Always does this.

_____ 1. Really listens to me.

_____ 2. Delegates new assignments and the authority to oversee them.

_____ 3. Thoroughly explains projects.

_____ 4. Cares about my growth and development.

_____ 5. Encourages me to take risks.

_____ 6. Respects me.

_____ 7. Gives me credit on projects I've contributed to.

_____ 8. Creates a positive work setting.

_____ 9. Knows his/her job.

_____ 10. Supports my actions and decisions.

_____ 11. Asks for my input.

_____ 12. Treats all employees fairly.

_____ 13. Gives specific, timely feedback on an ongoing basis.

_____ 14. Motivates me.

_____ 15. Enforces policies equitably.

_____ 16. Is able to explain organization's goals.

_____ 17. Helps me write good, challenging objectives.

_____ 18. Keeps me informed of pertinent company information.

_____ 19. Is consistent.

_____ 20. Appreciates my efforts.

■ ■ ■ ■ ■ ■ ■

360-Degree Feedback

360-degree Feedback is an evaluation and feedback approach that comes from all directions—above, below, and on all sides. Typically one employee is evaluated by the supervisor(s), peers, subordinates, customers, and possibly others. Also called Multi-Rater Feedback, this appraisal is the most comprehensive and costly. It also provides the broadest range of employee performance feedback. It tends to consolidate peer evaluations, upward appraisals, and self-reviews. But because feedback comes from all directions, there is risk of rater bias and varying focus. A manager, for example, may focus on results. Peers may focus on leadership potential or collegiality. Direct reports may look at whether they are included in decision-making.

Coworker bias can also contaminate results. _Insight-mag.com_, the online magazine of the Illinois CPA Society, identified three steps for limiting the effect of coworker bias. These include ensuring the rater's anonymity for more accurate feedback, holding the reviewee accountable by focusing on specifics of behavior, and fostering a climate in which performance is a serious matter, including an appeal mechanism.[66]

Given the considerable cost and time, 360-degree appraisals can hurt more than they help, especially when performance measures stray from business objectives. They need to be administered for the right reasons. Jeff Seretan, HR head of a San Francisco global investing firm, wrote that 360-degree appraisals should not be implemented "unless you can show that they are solving a problem or adding value." He uses the process to give senior executives feedback on their management style.[67]

Again, it is important to be completely clear about expectations. Everyone participating should be knowledgeable about the process and trained in assessing behavior and performance without bias. Documenting is important. And decisions about how the information is to be used—for development purposes, to justify a raise or bonus, etc.—must be made early on—*before* the appraisal occurs. How the employee receives the feedback is another important training topic.

■ ■ ■ ■ ■ ■ ■ ■ ■ ■ ■ ■

360-degree Appraisals[67]

Implement 360-degree feedback for the right reasons:

- ▣ Assess the cost of the program.
- ▣ Focus on business goals and strategy.
- ▣ Do not rely solely on 360-degree feedback.
- ▣ Get support at all levels of the organization.
- ▣ Train people in giving and receiving feedback.
- ▣ Create an "action plan" for each employee based on the feedback.

■ ■ ■ ■ ■ ■ ■

Automated Appraisals

The amount of time required to develop appraisals is an almost universal criticism. Already overloaded with paperwork, managers and employees are not looking for more. The time-consuming nature of good appraisals is one reason why it's so popular to just get through them...fast.

Jenni Lehman, research director of Gartner Group, wrote that "filling out forms, routing, and tracking is a nightmare" and that online appraisals can help. She recommends that, in choosing a performance appraisal package, companies know their goals, desired product features, and results.

"Companies have to be careful," Lehman cautioned, "because there's a real difference between having a robust application to help you manage and improve your performance reviews, and a Web-based process that just automates the process."[68]

A government agency has also automated the appraisal process. With the aim of reducing employee perceptions of inequity and favoritism, seven standards and evaluation criteria were developed. The same standards apply to everyone. Additional standards were developed for managers, supervisors, and team leaders. To help supervisors assess employees' progress in meeting goals and training, job descriptions and training history were linked to the appraisal. Pop-up screens were added to ensure that essential information would be included in mid-year evaluations. Both managers and employees responded enthusiastically to the automated approach, and there were improvements in timeliness and number of completed appraisals.

Just automating a poor appraisal tool will not boost timeliness or ease the process. It's still crucial to have clearly defined goals, performance standards that are understood and tied to the business plan, and action plans for dealing with any performance shortfalls. But once these elements are firmly in place, automating can make the process easier. A well-developed system can promote attention to training, performance gaps, and the need for course corrections. Training is a must if the system is to be fully utilized.

People With Special Challenges

Perception is probably the biggest workplace factor facing employees with particular challenges.

In a 1998 study, researchers asked:

1. How negative stereotypes would affect performance, evaluations and expectations, and whether team members would choose to have a person with a disability on their team; and

2. Whether the negative bias would be greater in performance evaluation, expectations and choice of team member if potential rewards were dependent on everyone's input.

In response to the first question, they found that disability had no effect on performance evaluations. Evaluators accurately assessed performance ratings and expectations. In response to the second question, they did find some negative stereotypes, most likely because respondents believed there might be unfavorable consequences for other team members.[69]

These findings have implications for the manager of a person with a disability. Although the researchers provide many caveats, it is clear that, just as with all perceptions, the view of how the employee is going to affect a situation when other self-interests are in play is a factor. This perception may have an impact on expectations for future performance. These, in turn, might have implications for the quality of coaching and performance correction interventions.

Education is a significant part of the performance appraisal. It should focus on abilities and the contributions that every employee has to offer. Too often stereotypes drive assumptions about how much an employee can accomplish, how much an employee can improve performance, and whether the employee can be a valuable member of a team. Acting to eliminate or minimize the impact of these stereotypes is the most responsible approach to take.

Aging Workforce Is "Booming"

"Boomers want to problem solve. Ask Nancy Boomer how she would handle XYZ if it arose in her workday."[70] Given that baby boomers are hitting their 50s, often with gaping holes in retirement savings, the workforce will benefit from millions of problem solvers in the decade to come. Perhaps even longer. Indications are that large numbers of boomers aren't necessarily planning to retire at age 65. In Human Resource Management, John M. Ivancevich wrote that boomers seek "assignments that allow them to learn and receive recognition for good work. Treat boomers as equals, and take authority-like commands out of the conversation."[71]

Raised with Vietnam, Watergate, television and assassinations, boomers tend not to be as trusting as the previous generation, but theirs is a generation that will continue to be vital, energetic, and involved. Boomers can thrive on step-by-step progress and clear sequences to success. Partner with boomers in developing performance appraisals, jointly structure a blueprint for the next evaluation cycle, build in victories along the way, and toss challenges right back for their recommendations.

The benefits to be reaped are considerable. As previously noted, in 1990 workers aged 55 or older comprised 11.9 percent of employees in private industry. In 2000, the number rose to 12.9 percent. The estimate by 2010 is 16.9 percent.[72]

Gen Xers

"Over the years, Generation X workers have gotten a bad rap for being self-absorbed, disloyal, and unwilling to pay their dues. This stereotype has led managers to take a very short-term approach to developing their career paths. But a study commissioned by Deloitte & Touche LLP and The Corporate State found that Gen Xers want a work environment that is 'stable' and 'clearly structured.'"[73]

Margaret Lack, principal and co-founder of The Millennium Group International, LLC in Virginia, wrote that "The key to Gen X appraisals is simple: Remember who the audience is!" According to Lack, Gen Xers place a high priority on self-reliance, independence, and work/life balance. They are goal-oriented and achievement focused, meaning that supervisors would be wise to develop a self-directed work environment, engaging the employee in targeting priorities and goals.

Because of this achievement orientation, it is important that Gen Xers see results, feel challenged, and learn new, marketable skills. As a rule, Gen Xers will want coaching. The ongoing nature of performance management will be appealing. Gen Xers tend to be flexible, technologically savvy and out-of-the-box thinkers. Lack advised customizing the appraisal process, with collaborative goal-setting to address self-management and achievement needs. Goals can be developed with continuing milestones so that results can be experienced early and often. "Stretch goals" can be tailored for particular challenges—this is a generation that was raised on games. Coaching, mentoring, and frequent, fast feedback will, according to Lack, provide value-added.

■ ■ ■ ■ ■ ■ ■ ■ ■ ■ ■ ■

Managing Gen Xers[74]

Adapted from Mary Ellen Rodgers, National Director for the Advancement of Women, Deloitte & Touche:

- ▣ Make Xers feel valuable.
- ▣ Help Xers develop various career paths.
- ▣ Allow Xers to be entrepreneurs within the organization.
- ▣ Communicate about fit with organizational vision and goals.
- ▣ Encourage mentoring.

■ ■ ■ ■ ■ ■ ■

Here Comes Generation Y

Generation Y is "up for any challenge ('bring it on' may well be the motto), and they have an astonishing amount of expertise in technology....They work well in team environments," wrote Joanne Sujansky in *Workforce Magazine*. Generation Y will number 80 million, and their considerable volume makes retaining them a top HR priority.[75]

Sujansky wrote that members of Generation Y "live to be trained" and want to be asked "their ideas and contributions." They should be given "opportunities to move up... They want to know how their work fits into a company's big picture." [Employers] should make sure that corrective feedback is balanced with praise. "Catch them doing something right, and reward them when you do...[they] absolutely thrive on recognition."[76] Generation Y will look for work assignments that are a cut apart, not just standard fare.

Eric Chester, an active speaker on "Generation Why," observed that Generation Y is "better educated, more creative and far more techno-savvy than those who have come before them. Employers can expect them to refuse to blindly conform to traditional standards and time-honored institutions."[77]

■ ■ ■ ■ ■ ■ ■ ■ ■ ■ ■ ■

Welcoming Generation Y

▣ Communicate the big picture.

▣ Motivate team-building.

▣ Create cool work assignments.

▣ Invite ideas.

▣ Balance correction with praise.

■ ■ ■ ■ ■ ■ ■

The Case for Ditching Appraisals
By Michael Strand

11

Here is Edward Bear, coming downstairs now, bump, bump, bump, on the back of his head... It is, as far as he knows, the only way of coming downstairs, but sometimes he feels that there really is another way, if only he could stop bumping for a moment and think of it. And then he feels that perhaps there isn't.

—A. A. Milne, author of the internationally best selling "Pooh" series, dramatist, novelist, and humorist

When something doesn't work, we usually want to fix it. Performance appraisals are an excellent example. For many organizations and HR professionals, fixing appraisals has become an enduring crusade. The hope is that somewhere out there exists the right model or formula to make performance appraisals work.

As Peter Scholtes put it: "If something is demonstrably the wrong thing to do ... you don't necessarily need an alternative in order to cease doing it. In order to stop beating your head against the wall, you don't need something else to beat your head against."[1]

Performance appraisals presume a fair and consistent process for evaluating and documenting worker performance. But in practice, do they measure up? Are appraisals a help or a hindrance? Do they facilitate employee motivation, or just create obstacles? Can the many concerns that exist be adequately fixed? Should the process itself be scraped? If so, what are better alternatives?

Because the process is human, it's also imperfect. The process is about perception—a supervisor's perception of an employee's performance and the employee's perception of the accuracy and fairness of the process. Folded into this process are three significant variables:

1. Supervisor's feelings, understanding, knowledge, and observations of an employee's performance.

2. Working conditions under which employees must perform, including priorities, concurrent activities, autonomy, creativity, resources, perhaps luck.

3. Employee perception of procedural and distributive justice— is the process (procedural) and the outcome (distributive) fair?[2]

Many factors contribute to this perceptual overlay:

Performance Scores/Errors

The performance appraisal process generally results in an overall rating or score. But there are multiple opportunities to err that can undermine this score. Unless the appraisal criteria are somewhat simplistic, such as a "go/no-go" approach to management by objectives, a narrative is needed to justify the performance assessment or score. But too often this narrative does not result in a consistent quantitative translation. If, for example, a supervisor's appraisal narrative were to be shared with perhaps a half-dozen HR professionals, the outcome is likely to result in different scores. Is it a 3.1, 3.3, or only a 2.7 level of performance? Supporting documentation may clearly differentiate a level 5 performance from a level 2, but a more definitive graduation for grading more tightly is usually not available and, if so, hardly consistent.

Although meant to be a fair representative of an employee's overall performance, susceptibility to one or several human errors puts the outcome of the entire appraisal process at risk. In fact, one of the major sources of errors is mistakes made by the rater.[3] As described in Chapter 6, there are at least 16 rating errors. Most well-intended supervisors probably don't know they are even making errors. Whether positive or negative, supervisors can also be perceiving performance rating as a means to justify prior interaction with employees instead of being a more objective reflection of performance over an entire rating cycle.

Lake Wobegon Syndrome

Just as in Garrison Keillor's fictional Lake Wobegon, where all children are deemed to be above average, some supervisors perceive goodness in every cubicle. This tendency to subjectively give employees high performance ratings is another form of rating error. Since favorable appraisals often lead to pay increases, and there is generally a limited pool of funds available for this purpose, organizations may impose a structure to limit the number of high ratings a supervisor may award. One example is a forced distribution (10 percent at outstanding; 40 percent at above average, etc.) that limits high ratings. Another is a zero sum game with a target performance increase of perhaps four percent. Every five percent increase must be balanced by a three percent increase. Such force-fit systems hinder a supervisor's understandable desire to reward loyal workers.

A related problem is that workers often believe they merit high ratings. In one study, 98 percent of workers believed they were above average compared to their coworkers. Another study revealed that 80 percent of workers thought they were in the top quarter. A broad study of workers across a variety of jobs showed that almost 60 percent objected to any rating that was less then the highest possible score.[4] Thus a lower than expected rating can be destructive to an employee's self esteem.

If a performance appraisal system were truly unbiased, accurate in measuring performance and statistically correct, 50 percent of employees would learn they are below average. Will this help them? Will this improve anything? Some who are classified as below average may resign themselves to their fate. Others will see such a classification as clear evidence that managers are hopelessly incompetent. [But perhaps the below average person will be motivated to improve performance in the next year.] Maybe they will be lucky, appear to do better, and be ranked above average, in which case their below average slot will open up and someone else will fill it.[5]

Changing Workplaces

New roles for supervisors and changing workplace circumstances can make it even more difficult for supervisors to observe and accurately assess worker performance. Yet we continue to expect a great deal from supervisors, holding them responsible for administering an overloaded appraisal process that rolls together ratings, feedback, improvement goals, development, training plans, pay-raise decisions and the triggering of disciplinary measures.[6]

In the past, supervisors tended to have fewer direct reports, subordinates were at the same work location, and the supervisor's primary responsibility was to supervise. Supervisors also tended to rise through the ranks, giving them the knowledge and experience to understand what their subordinates did and what it took to accomplish it. For budgetary and productive reasons, there has been a trend to reduce management layers. The result is often an increased burden on the first line supervisor. Consequently, the supervisor has responsibility over more people, employees may be supervised from afar (telecommuting or remote work locations), the supervisor may have little or no experience or expertise in the subordinate's work, and the primary role is often not one of supervision but as the emerging "working" supervisor responsible for piles of administrative and related details.

Angst Level

Like disciplinary action and involuntary termination, the anticipation and preparation of a performance appraisal produces an emotional anguish or "angst-level." Performance appraisal causes negative emotional states such as worry, depression, stress, and anguish on the part of those giving as well as those receiving appraisals.[7] Writing the narrative can be an onerous chore. How can it be instructive without being too critical? Should there be as many compliments as criticisms? And what if the employee disagrees with an observation or conclusion?

As a technique to minimize surprises, the appraised employee is often asked to first complete a self-appraisal identifying accomplishments and problems of the past year. This puts the worker in the awkward position of deciding how boastful or critical to be, and how much is in his or her best interest to reveal.

The Communication: Complete and return this document and then we will review your self-assessment along with my evaluation of your performance at the performance appraisal session next week.

The Message: Tell me what you are thinking and then I tell you what your performance accomplishments and failures really are.

Often an employee's primary goal is to just get through the process while maintaining one's dignity. For the more enterprising employee, he or she strives to maximize the carrots and minimize the stick and, occasionally, at the expense of other employees, use the old blame game method of deflecting criticism.

"[The performance appraisal system] devours staggering amounts of time and energy; it depresses and demotivates people; it destroys trust and teamwork and, adding insult to injury, it delivers little demonstrable value at great cost."[8]

Timing...It Never Seems Right

Organizations have to determine how frequently to conduct performance reviews. Should the review be distributed throughout the year, such as on the employee's anniversary date? Or should it be concentrated to a few weeks each year when everyone throughout the organization is reviewed?

The anniversary date approach spreads the angst, in lower doses, throughout the year. It also allows for chronic tardiness in completing the appraisal. This necessitates retroactive pay adjustments for performance systems linked to pay-for-performance.

As an organization-wide activity requiring everyone's attention, the annual review facilitates timely completion of reviews. It is argued that this concentrated method yields more accurate performance comparisons because all reviews are done at approximately the same time. However, the organization may be so preoccupied during the weeks of performance review that other mission-critical activities receive less timely attention. An annual review also gives supervisors an excuse not to provide timely feedback. Too often the supervisor will put off communicating a criticism until review time, either to delay an undesirable chore or to accumulate topics for the yearly appraisal session. Eliminating the appraisal takes away the excuse to procrastinate.

The Tail Wagging the Dog

Proponents of performance appraisals cite the legal necessities of documenting performance. They underscore the critical need to safeguard against lawsuits, determine whom to discipline, and decide which employees to include in a reduction-in-force. They argue that the performance appraisal can provide the documentation necessary to adequately address such serious situations. However, because of problems with distorted ratings cited above and in Chapter 6, the performance appraisal itself may be incomplete or erroneous and, as a result, be contested. As detailed in Chapter 9, it may even prove to be harmful evidence. Secondly, maintaining an appraisal process for all workers in order to address the potential problems of just a few does not make much sense. Poor performers probably constitute less than 10 percent of the work force, so why incur the expense of keeping book on the entire work force?[9]

> **The Communication**: Signing this evaluation does not necessarily mean you agree with it. You may provide any relevant comments in the space below. If you fail to sign this evaluation, your supervisor may call in a witness to confirm you have received it."

> **The Message**: We want to prove you received this document, and we will lock it in our files in case we have to use it against you later.

Why Do We Keep Doing Them?

Appraisals persist as management tools for several reasons. They feed us the illusion that we are tangibly taking action to institute control, focus energies, measure performance, and bring about accountability in accomplishing desired results. Appraisal gives us documentation of people being encouraged to improve. This feels good because, by holding conversations about improvement and filling out forms, we believe we are making people accountable and getting improvement. This alluring but false impression has enabled appraisals to survive despite alternative attempts to apply new philosophical approaches to the management of workers.[10]

Top management wants performance appraisals to be imposed throughout the organization because it demonstrates that there is some direction and control over employee performance. Because top management is physically removed from real work and real workers, the only forms of motivation and control they have to offer anyone are externally imposed motivation and control, namely performance appraisals.[11]

Furthermore, management believes that appraisals offer a perceived linear way to control performance. Because there often is a fundamental distrust of workers, management needs some objectives to ensure that work is being done. They have an implicit notion that they must try to fit people into their system, department, or company.[12]

The old system of offering carrots and brandishing sticks lends itself to a managerial "formula" that requires little knowledge of human behavior and less challenge than time-consuming employee one-on-one communication, interactive discussion of system improvements, and basic understanding of motivation and employee recognition. While many organizations are reaching out and stretching hard to foster the best possible climate for their employees, including assessing and reassessing how performance appraisals are conducted, many others stay stuck in conducting business as usual. In many of these organizations, performance appraisals also stay stuck, as perfunctory exercises that serve minimal value or, in fact, undercut their good intent.

■ ■ ■ ■ ■ ■ ■ ■ ■ ■ ■ ■

No Appraisals or Merit Pay

Glenroy, Inc., with 100-plus employees, concluded in the 80s that its performance ratings were "subjective," and employee feedback was an "illusion." Glenroy, which produces flexible packing material in Wisconsin, totally ditched its performance appraisal system. Since without an appraisal system, Glenroy had no "formalized feedback process," feedback activity reverted to a day-to-day process. Merit pay was eliminated because it was "an obstacle to getting people to cooperate and collaborate." Pay increase became directly tied to the market. "After more than a decade without appraisals and merit pay, the company and its workforce seem quite pleased."[13]

■ ■ ■ ■ ■ ■ ■

Better Options

Feedback Without Judgment

One key is to establish feedback without judgment. "Judgment is the explicit or implicit attribution that the other person is right, wrong, good or bad."[14] Traditional performance appraisal is about judgment—a supervisor's judgment of the successes and failures of a worker. Judgment is typically a one-way initiation that is often interpreted by the receiver as an act of control over the person being evaluated rather than a welcome suggestion of behavior improvement. There is a presumption that the "problem" is with the person being evaluated, not with the system that may be the root cause of the poor performance. In contrast to judgment, feedback's purpose is to improve the system. Feedback must be in the form of data. W. Edwards Deming observed that performance appraisals became popular because it was easier for supervisors to rate workers than discover the cause(s) of the "problem." Deming encourages supervisors to conduct a long interview with each worker "at least once a year, not for criticism, but for help and better understanding on the part of everybody."[15]

"The semi-annual or annual appraisal is not a particularly effective stimulus to learning. It provides 'feedback' about behavior at a time remote from the behavior itself. People do learn and can change as a result of feedback. But the most effective feedback occurs immediately after the behavior."[16] Behavioral feedback (negative and positive) should occur as soon as a supervisor is aware of it.

■ ■ ■ ■ ■ ■ ■ ■ ■ ■ ■ ■

The Annual Sit-down

With 16,000 employees, Wheaton Franciscan Services in Illinois abolished performance appraisals in the early 1990s and embarked on a campaign of developing solid communications skills for all leaders. At one annual "sit-down" conversation, the supervisor and employee "looked together at the work and their working relationship. A simple form provides a context for the conversation, focusing on objectives, changing roles, long-term aspirations, a personal learning plan, and eliminating barriers." Since the completed form, initially a part of each employee's personnel file, "perpetuated the stigma of the formal appraisal process," Wheaton made the form optional in 1998. The less formalized approach made employees more comfortable with the process.[17]

■ ■ ■ ■ ■ ■ ■

■ ■ ■ ■ ■ ■ ■ ■ ■ ■ ■ ■

Feedback vs. Judgment

▣ Are there data involved in the exchange, or merely judgment?

▣ Is the review from one part of the system to another part of the system? Or is it from a boss to a subordinate?

▣ Is it directly related to improvement of the process, or is it related to the accountability of the individuals or groups?"[18]

Feedback should address the system through effective communication and the input of people within the system:

- Think systems, not individual employee performance. Get everyone to think about the work processes, how they interrelate, and outcomes that best serve the customer.

- Promote systems thinking. Get everyone to focus on the customer and the interrelated activities and events that serve customers well.

- Strive to control the systems. Get everyone to control and improve the systems, instead of systems controlling the workforce.

- Strive to create and maintain outstanding systems. Create high expectations for outstanding systems, achieving "excellent results, with the ordinary efforts of average people."[19]

▦ ▦ ▦ ▦ ▦ ▦ ▦

Shift Responsibility From Supervisor to Employee

We need to rethink and reengineer the employee's role in the system. The goal is to shift (or at least share) responsibility and authority so that the employee is vested in his or her own professional development. This stimulates a more meaningful and accepting feedback process.

The General Motors Powertrain division (26,000 employees) created a new feedback process where the worker would "choose feedback givers from a group that included supervisors, coworkers, and subordinates." Forms were completed by the selected feedback group and summarized by the employee's immediate supervisor; no ratings, no scores, just narrative. Employees liked the idea of getting feedback from peers and subordinates.

And it shifted responsibility to the employee to decide when the feedback would take place and from whom it would come.[20]

"Lasting change will come only when employees take on a new view of themselves, accepting that they are adults responsible for their own growth, development, and self-worth. The ultimate goal is to help people attain an authentic and energized commitment to the organization and its goal of efficiently providing quality service and products."[21]

■ ■ ■ ■ ■ ■ ■ ■ ■ ■ ■ ■ ■

Appraisals Out/Sales Up

Since 1991, Gallery Furniture Company in Houston, Texas, has achieved a four-fold increase in sales. That's the year it stopped paying commissions to sales staff and completely dropped performance appraisal and merit increases for all 200 employees. Instead, according to Gallery's VP, employees are "appraised every day as they need it. We talk to people and listen to them. We help them if they need it, but mostly we try to make work fun." At Gallery Furniture, management believes that performance appraisals just get in the way of communication.[22]

▩ ▩ ▩ ▩ ▩ ▩ ▩

Meet Higher-Level Worker Needs

We need to develop workplace methodologies and conditions (employee feedback, involvement, development, and job structure) that focus on the higher-level needs identified by Abraham Maslow. These needs, in ascending order, identify unfulfilled worker needs in most organizations.

▣ **Social needs**: the need for meaningful relationships with others, for recognition by supervisors, peers, and subordinates, and by holding a respected position in the group.

▣ **Esteem needs**: the need for feeling good about oneself, for self-respect and self-confidence, and a sense of achievement and competence.

▣ **Self-actualization needs**: the need to fulfill one's potential, for continued self-development, for intellectual challenge and achievement.

Because it is often difficult for organizations to develop mechanisms to address these needs, they are seldom satisfied and go unfulfilled, leaving a huge void in the needs of workers. But some companies seize the opportunity to meet these needs. Entre Computer Systems designs and implements information system networks in Lansing, Michigan. In the early 1990s, it eliminated performance appraisal and pay-for-performance plans. The company reserves an amount equal to 10 percent of each of its 60 employees' salaries for training and development. On a voluntary basis, workers meet with their supervisors each year to discuss development and how those training dollars will be used. Through this commitment to employee development, Entre is devoting resources to meet the higher-level needs of its workers.[23]

■ ■ ■ ■ ■ ■ ■ ■ ■ ■ ■ ■

What About Pay?

People should get paid approximately what they would get paid for doing the same work elsewhere.[24] To learn about market rates, methodologies for major compensation initiatives can follow these guidelines:

1. Identify methods to regularly determine the market rate of each position.

2. Determine compensation relative to the market rate (median, 10 percent above median, 75th percentile, etc.).

3. Adjust individual pay when it is significantly below the market rate, or not reflective of employee's experience.[25]

■ ■ ■ ■ ■ ■ ■

Get Rid of Rewards Except When...

There is evidence that, under certain circumstances, pay incentives do motivate improved performance. But just in the short run. Soon the effect of the incentive wears off and employee performance returns to the old "unmotivated" ways. Money can motivate when work is of little importance and dollars are an effective replacement of value, and when work is quantity driven and a good job consists of producing more of something or completing it faster.[26]

In some situations, the traditional performance appraisal may also be appropriate. Typically, these are temporary or one-time circumstances, such as the following:

◻ **Probation.** New employees go through a probationary period to determine if there is a good match between the worker and the position. Throughout and upon completion of the probationary period, a performance assessment checklist can be helpful in identifying competencies and justifying a change from probationary to regular status.

◻ **Unacceptable Performance.** Workers whose performance has become substandard and who have not responded favorably to counseling, may be placed in a probationary disciplinary status. Written performance expectations and performance standards may be helpful in defining specific objectives to be achieved to continue in the position.

◻ **At Employee's Request.** Workers may prefer an appraisal, either as a way of comparison to previous activities or as documentation to support job accomplishment claims to a prospective employer.

According to Alfie Kohn, "not a single controlled study has ever found that the use of rewards produces a long-term improvement in the quality of the work. In fact, experimental simulations continue to suggest that the opposite is true. Psychologists have discovered, for example, that supervisors tended to provide less informational feedback to employees and were 'more controlling in their style of supervision when their job included administering rewards.'"[27]

Research has demonstrated that rewards can actually have a detrimental effect on productivity, constrain quality, stifle creativity, and undermine intrinsic motivation. Kohn cites scores of studies that substantiate these conclusions in his book, *Punished by Rewards: The Trouble with Gold Stars, Incentive Plans, A's, Praise, and Other Bribes.*

The Communication: "Do this and you'll get that."

The Message: The task is not of value in and of itself because I must give you something in exchange for doing it.

A Lesson in Trust

In the mid-1980s, the Milwaukee-based Falk Corporation, in the context of evaluating its policies and practices, decided to determine what portion of its employees were trustworthy and what portion were untrustworthy. After developing criteria for both categories, the managers assessed each employee. The result: at least 95 percent of its employees were considered trustworthy. Perhaps five percent of the workforce was considered untrustworthy. Organizational leaders concluded that their policies, practices, and procedures were written for the five percent that were considered untrustworthy. Among other changes, its 175-word bereavement leave policy was reduced to the following: "If you require time off due to a death of a friend or family member, make arrangements with your supervisor." The offshoot: under the new policy, the total number of days used for bereavement leave was just 47 percent of the days used under the old policy.[28]

■■■■■■■■■■■■

Topping the Satisfaction List

The 500-person police department in Madison, Wisconsin stopped doing traditional appraisals for most personnel in 1989-90, replacing them with a system of individual goal-setting, leadership-setting, and employee involvement. The approach even extends to officers choosing the sergeants they want to work with, sergeants choosing lieutenants, and so on. A U.S. Department of Justice study of 12 metropolitan police departments found Madison police to be the highest in satisfaction level among citizens, regardless of racial community. Each year, the department receives more than 1,000 applications for its two dozen openings. University of Wisconsin Credit Union, also in Madison, replaced its appraisal system with an array of elective, flexible coaching tools and formats. The result has been improved employee satisfaction and a dramatic reduction in turnover.[29]

■ ■ ■ ■ ■ ■ ■

■■■■■■■■■■■

"Time Better Spent"

The argument against doing traditional appraisals was persuasive enough to capture the attention of Bruce Mallory, vice president of a 200-person Eugene, Oregon credit union. Scrapping the firm's entire appraisal system, management opted to give individual managers an annual financial pool. Bonuses and raises are awarded as managers deem fair. Managers meet with their teams regularly and document the discussions. Four years after implementing this approach, Mallory's only regret is that he didn't try it sooner. "We figure that we've saved at least $350,000 in time spent alone. It doesn't mean that we're spending any less time with people. But it's time better spent. It's managing people differently, rather than managing the paper flow."[30]

■ ■ ■ ■ ■ ■ ■

Dare to Change the Landscape

To dump performance appraisals is a daring move. The corporate establishment is married to them, supervisors are hardened by them, and employees are conditioned to having them. But "there is no valid research to demonstrate that an organization is better off for having used performance evaluation."[31]

"Appraisals continue because everyone else does it—it is part of the landscape of management. And it fits our linear way of thinking. In Western society, we have difficulty in looking at the circularity of things, indirect causes, and unintended consequences—we look for the direct line. If there is a problem, we tell the person he screwed up, instead of thinking of the circular and contextual causes and the design of the system. Poor performance issues are often about fit. Most performance problems are not about people who are duds, but about people who are in the wrong job or with the wrong company."[32]

"To break away from appraisals, first, companies must have the guts to break away from what everyone else is doing. Second, they must create alternative ways to deal with performance and understand performance. Foremost, they must focus on high-performance systems—the organizational culture, what the customer wants, goals, people having a voice, units having information and autonomy, and feedback from actions and the results of work units and the company. These actions will help people be more performance-oriented and help them care about performance and high standards. These strategies will make appraisals unnecessary."[33]

If organizations redirected just a portion of the time spent on "fixing" hopelessly broken appraisal systems to meeting higher-level needs, they would have much happier employees, committed to improving systems, and producing higher quality products and services. If a practice appears anti-productive, and organizations believe it's not working, why not just stop practicing it? It's essential to be clear about needs—and alternatives that will genuinely fill them.

Chapter Notes

Introduction

[1] Susan Parks, "Improving Workplace Performance: Historical and Theoretical Contexts," *Monthly Labor Review*, May 1995, 20.

[2] Angelo S. DeNisi and Ricky W. Griffin, *Human Resource Management*, (Massachusetts: Houghton Mifflin Company, 2001), 356.

[3] Bill L. Hopkins and Thomas C. Mawhinney, eds., *Pay for Performance*, (New York: The Haworth Press, Inc., 1992), 17.

[4] J. Lawrie, "Prepare For a Performance Appraisal," *Personnel Journal*, April 1990, Vol. 69, 132-136.

[5] Marjorie G. Derven, "The Paradox of Performance Appraisals," *Personnel Journal*, February 1990, Vol. 69, 107-111.

[6] Bob Nelson, *1001 Ways to Reward Employees*, (New York: Workman Publishing, 1994), XV.

Chapter 1

[1] Oren Harari, *The Leadership Secrets of Colin Powell*, (New York: McGraw-Hill, 2002), 259.

[2] Peter F. Drucker, *The Practice of Management*, (New York: Harper Business, 1986), 312.

[3] David Butcher, "It Takes Two to Review," *Management Today*, London, England: Haymarket Publishing LTD, November 2002, 54-59.

[4] Hopkins and Mawhinney, 7.

[5] Ingo W. Schroder, "The Political Economy of Common Destinies in the American Indian Southwest," *Journal of the Southwest*, Spring 2002, 3.

[6] C. Andrew Gerstle, "Heroic Honor: Chikamatsu and the Samurai Ideal," *Harvard Journal of Asiatic Studies*, December 1997, 307.

[7] Paula Span, "Marriage At First Sight," *Washington Post Magazine*, February 23, 2003, 20.

[8] Dennis M. Daley, *Strategic Human Resource Management*, (New Jersey: Prentice Hall, 2001), 55.

[9] Joseph LeDoux, *The Emotional Brain*, (New York: Touchstone/Simon & Schuster, 1986), 36.

[10] Ibid., 131.

[11] Kenneth A. Kovach, *Strategic Human Resources Management*, (Maryland: University Press of America, 1996), 1-4.

[12] Wayne F. Cascio, *Managing Human Resources*, 6th ed., (New York: McGraw-Hill Higher Education, 2003), 330.

[13] Susan Heathfield, "Performance Appraisals Don't Work," *Human Resources* [home page online]; available from *www.humanresources.guide@about.com*; Internet; accessed June 2000.

[14] DeNisi, 309.

[15] Dennis R. Tesdell, "The Top Ten Fears That Keep People From Getting What They Want In Life," Adapted from *CoachVille Resource Center*, *www.coachville.com*, 1998.

[16] Kovach, 4.

Chapter 2

[1] John C. Maxwell, *The 17 Essential Qualities of A Team Player*, (Tennessee: Thomas Nelson Publishers, 2002), 105.

[2] Henry Mintzberg, *The Manager's Job*, (Massachusetts: Harvard Business School Press, 1998), 23.

[3] Matthew McKay, Martha Davis, and Patrick Fleming, *Messages*, (California: New Harbinger Publications, Inc., 1995), 167.

[4] Ibid., 45.

[5] Ibid., 47.

[6] Karen McKirchey, *Powerful Performance Appraisals*, (New Jersey: Career Press, 1998), 21.

[7] Marcus Buckingham and Curt Coffman, *First, Break All The Rules - What the World's Greatest Managers Do Differently*, (New York: Simon and Schuster, 1999), 226.

[8] Drucker, 307.

[9] H. Jackson Brown, Jr., ed., *A Father's Book of Wisdom*, (Tennessee: Rutledge Hill Press, 1988), 157.

[10] Edward T. Hall, *The Silent Language*, (New York: Anchor Books, 1990), 33-34.

[11] Nancy Branton, project manager of Minnesota Department of Natural Resources survey, as quoted in Bob Nelson, *1001 Ways*, 19.

Chapter 3

1 Dennis M. Daley, *Strategic Human Resource Management-People and Performance Management in the Public Sector*, (Upper Saddle River, NJ: Prentice Hall, 2002), 186.

2 John M. Ivancevich, 251, citing Mary N. Vinson (April 1996), "The Pros and Cons of 360-Degree Feedback: Making It Work," *Training and Development*, Vol. 50, Issue 4, 11-12.

3 Colleen O'Neill, quoted by Patricia V. Rivera in *The Dallas Morning News*, Jan 22, 2003.

4 J. Samuel Bois, *The Art of Awareness*, 3rd ed., (Iowa: Wm. C. Brown Publishers, 1979), 240.

5 Edwin Newman, *Strictly Speaking*, (New York: The Bobbs-Merrill Company, 1974), 151.

6 Daley, 56.

7 Daley, 57.

8 Wayne R. Mondy et al, *Human Resource Management* (8th ed.), (New Jersey: Prentice Hall, 2002), 110.

9 Norman R. Augustine, *Reshaping an Industry*, (Massachusetts: Harvard Business School Press, 1998), 182-83.

10 Maxwell, 138.

11 Buckingham and Coffman, 151.

12 Harari, 33.

13 George R. Dreher and Thomas W. Dougherty, *Human Resource Strategy - A Behavioral Perspective for the General Manager*, (New York: McGraw-Hill/ Irwin, 2002), 158.

14 T. Redman et al., "Performance Appraisal in an NHS Hospital," *Human Resource Management Journal*, Vol. 10, No. 1, 2002, 48-62.

15 McKay et al, 24-25.

16 Ibid., 35.

17 D. Dryer, J. P. Dittman, and T. Farris, "General Motors and Whirlpool: Two Approaches for Developing Performance Benchmarks," *HR Focus*, Vol. 77, Issue 6, June 2000, 7-8.

18 Tony Moglia, *Partners in Performance, Successful Performance Management*, (California: Crisp Publications, Inc., 1997), 21.

Chapter 4

1 Paul Lukas, *Fortune Small Business*, The Great American Company, "Kellogg: Champion of Breakfast," March 19, 2003.

2 Paul Lukas, *Fortune Small Business*, The Great American Company, "Holiday Inns: Be My Guest," March 19, 2003.

3 Paul Lukas, *Fortune Small Business*, The Great American Company, "Johnson & Johnson: Medicine Men," March 19, 2003.

4 Ibid.

5 Maxwell, 93.

[6] John P. Kotter, "Winning at Change" *Leader to Leader*, 10 (Fall 1998): 27-33.

[7] Paul Lukas, *Fortune Small Business*, The Great American Company, "UPS: The Whole Package," March 19, 2003.

[8] Louis V. Gerstner, *Who Says Elephants Can't Dance*, (New York: Harper Business, 2002), dedication page.

[9] Charles M. Farkas and Suzy Wetlaufer, *The Way Chief Executive Officers Lead*, (Boston, MA: Harvard Business Review on Leadership, Harvard Business School Press, 1998), 28.

[10] Discussion moderated by Harris Collingwood and Julia Kirby, *All in a Day's Work*, (Boston, MA: Harvard Business Review on Breakthrough Leadership, Harvard Business School Press, 2001), 63.

[11] James C. Collins and Jerry I. Porras, *Building Your Company's Vision*, (Boston, MA: Harvard Business Review on Change, Harvard Business School Press, 1998), 30.

[12] Ibid., 26.

[13] Drucker, 146.

[14] Robert S. Kaplan and David P. Norton, *The Balanced Scorecard*, (Boston, MA: Harvard Business School Press, 1996), 202.

[15] Collins and Porras, 38-39.

[16] Farkas and Wetlaufer, 117-122.

[17] Mary Hayes, "Goal Oriented," *InformationWeek*, 930, March 10, 2003, 35.

[18] Ibid., 36.

[19] Omar Aguilar, "How Strategic Performance Management is Helping Companies Create Business Value," *Strategic Finance*, Vol. 87, Issue 7, January 2003, 48.

[20] Ibid., 49.

[21] Drucker, 64.

[22] Ibid., 124.

[23] J. Samuel Bois, *The Art of Awareness*, (Dubuque, Iowa: Wm. C. Brown Publishers, 1978), 289.

[24] Maxwell, 95.

[25] Stephen J. Brewer, "Aligning Human Capital in Achieving Business Goals and Strategic Objectives," SHRM White Paper, September, 2000, Reviewed March 2002.

[26] Jonathan A. Segal, "Fine-Tune Performance Appraisals to Make Them Effective—and Less Arduous," SHRM Managing Smart, 1 Quarter 2001.

[27] Collingwood and Kirby, 58.

[28] Raymond Noe, John Hollenbeck, Barry Gerhart, Patrick Wright, *Human Resource Management - Gaining a Competitive Advantage*, 3rd ed., (New York: McGraw-Hill/Irwin, 2000), 292.

[29] Ibid.

[30] Ivancevich, 261.

[31] Gerstner, 202.

[32] Aguilar, 49.

[33] Kaplan and Norton, 2.

34 Ibid.
35 Liz Fisher, "Thou Shalt Not Fail, Balanced Scorecard Implementation, 10 Commandments from KPMG", *Accountancy International*, September, 1998, Vol. 122, Issue 1261, cited in "Balanced Scorecard Basics on Implementation," by Valerie E. Pike, December 2000, Reviewed March 2002, SHRM White Paper.

Chapter 5

1 Hopkins and Mawhinney, 10.
2 Ivancevich, 71.
3 Thomas G. Moehrie, "The Evolution of Compensation in a Changing Economy," *Issue of Compensation and Working Conditions*, Bureau of Labor Statistics, Fall 2001, Vol. 6, Issue 3, 10.
4 Parks, 20.
5 Parks, as quoted from Walter Licht, "Studying Work: Personnel Policies in Philadelphia Firms, 1850 - 1950." Sanford Jacoby, ed., *Masters to Managers* (New York: Columbia University Press, 1991).
6 Sanford M. Jacoby, A Century of Human Resource Management, paper presented at 75th Anniversary Conference of Industrial Relations Counselors, Princeton University, September 11, 2001, 5.
7 Moehrie, 10.
8 Ibid.
9 Albert E. Schwenk and Jordan N. Pfuntner, "Compensation in the Later Part of the Century, *"Issue of Compensation and Working Conditions*, Vol. 6, Issue 3, Bureau of Labor Statistics, Fall 2001, 1.
10 Moehrie, 9.
11 Donald L. Caruth and Gail D. Handlogten, *Managing Compensation (and Understanding It Too)*, (Connecticut: Quorum Books, 2001), 1.
12 Ibid., 2, as quoted from Donald L. Caruth, *Compensation Management for Banks* (Boston, MA: Bankers Publishing, 1986), 7.
13 Ibid., 1.
14 Robert L. Mathis and John H Jackson, *Human Resources Management*, 10th ed., (Mason, OH: South-Western College Publications, 2003), 375.
15 Ibid.
16 Gerstner, 100-101.
17 Ibid.
18 Scott Hays, "Pros and Cons of Pay for Performance," *ZPG* [home page online]; available from *http://www.zigonperf.com/resources/pmnews/proscons.html*; Internet; accessed 14 April 2003.
19 Jeffrey Pfeffer, *Six Dangerous Myths About Pay*, (Boston, MA: Harvard Business Review on Managing People, Harvard Business School Press, 1999), 94.
20 Ibid.
21 J. Pfeffer, C. O'Reilly III, *Hidden Value: How Great Companies Achieve Extraordinary Results with Ordinary People*, (Boston, MA: Harvard Business School Press, 2000), 42-43.

[22] Terry Satterfield, "Speaking of Pay," *HR Magazine*, Vol. 48, No. 3, March 2003, 99-101.

[23] Ibid.

[24] Caruth as cite 11, 170, as quoted from *Compensation,* 6th ed., George T. Milkovich and Jerry M. Newman, (Boston, MA: McGraw-Hill/Irwin, 1999), 410-412.

[25] Satterfield, 99-101.

[26] Caruth, 45.

[27] Satterfield, 99-101.

[28] Ivancevich, 335-336.

[29] Lance A. Berger and Dorothy R. Berger, eds., *The Compensation Handbook*, 4th ed., (New York: McGraw-Hill, 1999), 132-133.

[30] Mathis, 373.

[31] James W. Smither, ed., *Performance Appraisal: State of the Art in Practice*, (San Francisco, CA: John Wiley & Sons, Inc., 1998), 506.

[32] Berger, 200.

[33] H. H. Altmansberger and M. Wallace, "Designing a GoalSharing Program." *American Compensation Association (ACA) Building Blocks*, Scottsdale, AZ, 1998.

[34] Caruth, 146.

[35] Ivancevich, 311.

[36] Scott Hays, "Pros and Cons of Pay for Performance," *ZPG* [home page online]; available from *http://www.zigonperf.com/resources/pmnews/proscons.html*; Internet; accessed 14 April 2003, quoting Alfie Kohn.

[37] Ibid.

[38] Hays,

[39] Pfeffer, 90.

[40] Pfeffer, 89-90.

[41] Jody Hoffer Gittell, *The Southwest Airlines Way*, (New York: McGraw-Hill, 2003), 141.

[42] Nelson, 3.

[43] Ibid., 104.

[44] Ibid.

Chapter 6

[1] Shimon L. Dolan and Denis Moran, "The Effects of Rater-Ratee Relationship on Ratee Perceptions of the Appraisal Process*,*" *Human Resource Management*, 8th ed., (New York: McGraw-Hill/Irwin, 2001), 337-351.

[2] Drucker, 81-82.

[3] DeNisi and Griffin, 250.

[4] DeNisi, 7.

[5] Sanford M. Jacoby, A Century of Human Resource Management, from a paper presented at the 75th Anniversary Conference of Industrial Relations Counselors, Princeton University, 11 September 2001.

[6] David Day et al., *HR Briefing*, (Aspen Publishers, July 1, 2002), 7.

[7] Jane Halpert, Midge Wilson, Julia Hickman, "Pregnancy as a Source of Bias in Performance Appraisals," *Journal of Organizational Behavior* 14 (1993), 655.

[8] William S. Swan, *How To Do a Superior Performance Appraisal*, (New York: John Wiley & Sons, 1991), 120.

[9] Ibid., 121.

[10] H. John Bernardin and Richard W. Beatty, *Performance Appraisal: Assessing Human Behavior at Work*, (Boston, MA: Kent Publishing, 1984), 140.

[11] E.D. Pulakos, "The Development of Training Programs to Increase Accuracy on Different Rating Forms," *Organizational Behavior and Human Decision Processes*, 38 (1986), 76-91.

[12] Jerry W. Hedge and Michael J. Kavanagh, "Improving the Accuracy of Performance Evaluations: Comparisons of Three Methods of Performance Appraiser Training," *Journal of Applied Psychology*, February 1988, Vol. 73, Issue 1, in *Human Resource Management* (8th ed.), John M. Ivancevich, McGraw-Hill/Irwin, NY, 2001, 268.

Chapter 7

[1] Maxwell, 1.

[2] Ibid., 77.

[3] Ibid., 78.

[4] Brian L. Davis et al., *The Successful Manager's Handbook - Development Suggestions for Today's Managers*, (Minneapolis, MN: Personnel Decisions International, 1992), 407.

[5] Adam M. Brandenburger and Barry J. Nalebuff, *Co-opetition*, (New York: Doubleday, 1996), 199.

[6] Ibid., 209.

[7] Peter R. Scholtes, "Total Quality or Performance Appraisal: Choose One," *National Productivity Review*, 349, Summer, 1993, Vol. 12, No. 3, Joiner Associates; Dov Eden, *Pygmalion in Management*, (Lexington, MA: Lexington Press, 1990).

[8] Ferdinand F. Fournies, *Coaching*, (New York: McGraw-Hill, 2000), 158.

[9] Ibid., 160-161.

[10] Bois, 345.

[11] Joseph C. Badaracco, Jr., *Leading Quietly*, (Boston, MA: Harvard Business School Press, 2002), 148.

[12] Badaracco, 5.

[13] Jim Collins, *Good To Great*, (New York: Harper Business, 2001), 88.

[14] Maxwell, 24.

[15] Fournies, 68.

[16] Ibid.

[17] Ibid., 177.

[18] Ibid.

[19] Davis et al., 288.

[20] Maxwell, 35.

[21] Maxwell, 8.

[22] Davis et al, 139.

[23] McKay et al, 48.

[24] Paul J. Jerome, *Coaching Through Effective Feedback - A Practical Guide to Successful Communication*, (California: Richard Chang Associates, Jossey-Bass/Pfeiffer, 1994), March 2000, viii, quoting Dr. John H. Reitmann.

[25] Ibid., 85.

[26] Ibid., 55.

[27] Ibid, 56.

[28] McKay et al, 48.

[29] Dr. Deborah Tannen, *That's Not What I Meant*, (New York: Ballantine Books, 1986), 61.

[30] McKay et al, 8-10.

[31] Adapted from Paul J. Jerome, *Coaching Through Effective Feedback - A Practical Guide to Successful Communication.*

Chapter 9

[1] Carlton v. Mystic Transportation, Inc. 202 F .3d 129 (2d Cir.).

[2] Other categories protected under some state and local laws include sexual orientation, marital status, political affiliation, personal appearance, and family responsibilities.

[3] *Burlington Indus., Inc v. Ellerth*, 524 U.S. 742 (1998).

[4] *Russell v. Principi*, 257 F. 3d 815 (D.C. Cir. 2001).

[5] *Brennan v. GTE Government Systems Corp.*, 150 F.3d 21 (1st Cir.).

[6] Rodriquez-Cuervos v. Wal-Mart Stores, Inc., 181 F3d 15 (1st Cir.).

[7] Protected activities are defined as: making a formal or informal complaint of discrimination; opposing a discriminatory work practice; and participating in either a discrimination investigation or court case.

Chapter 10

[1] Alvin Toffler, *Powershift*, (New York: Bantam Books, Bantam Doubleday Dell Publishing Group, 1990), 82.

[2] Ibid., 82.

[3] Ibid., 76.

[4] Ibid., 75.

[5] James A. Brickley et al., *Designing Organizations to Create Value*, (New York: McGraw-Hill Companies, 2003), 44.

[6] Ibid., 45.

[7] Table 5, Bureau of Labor Statistics, U.S. Department of Labor, Civilian Labor Force by Sex, Age, Race & Hispanic Origin 1990, 2000 and projected 2010 Civilian Population Survey.

[8] Joanne Sujansky, "The Critical Care and Feeding of Generation Y," *Workforce*, Vol. 81, Issue 5, Costa Mesa, CA., May, 2002, 15.

[9] Ibid.

[10] Susan Parks, "Improving Workplace Performance: Historical and Theoretical Contexts," *Monthly Labor Review*, May 1995, 20, quoting Sanford Jacoby, *Employing Bureaucracy: Masters to Managers: Historical and Comparative Perspectives on American Employers*, (New York: Columbia University Press, 1991), 15.

[11] "Keep Your Staff—Even Without the Big Pay Increases," *Accounting Office Management & amp; Administration Report*, available from *www.smartbiz.com/* article/view/176 [home page online]; Internet; accessed May 2003.

[12] Michael Schrage, "Shared Minds: The New Technologies of Collaboration," interview in *The Washington Post* by Don Oldenburg, March 12, 1991, E5.

[13] Ibid.

[14] Ibid.

[15] Alex Hiam, *Making Horses Drink*, (Irvine, CA: Entrepreneur Media, Inc., 2002), 76.

[16] Ibid., 84.

[17] Patrick J. Kiger, "Optimas 2001 - Vision: Frequent Employee Feedback Is Worth The Cost And Time," *Workforce*, Vol. 80, Issue 3, Costa Mesa, CA., March 2001, 62.

[18] Christopher J. Shinkman, "Performance Appraisal: A Positive Approach," *AFP Exchange*, Bethesda, MD, Mar/Apr 2001; Vol. 21, Issue 2, 78-80.

[19] Brickley, ed., 44.

[20] Davis et al, 429.

[21] Robert H. Schaffer and Harvey A. Thomson, "Successful Change Programs Begin with Results," *Harvard Business Review on Change*, January/February 1992, Vol. 70, Iss. 1, 80.

[22] Maxwell, 80.

[23] Ibid., 77.

[24] Editors of Wall Street Journal, *Boss Talk—Top CEOs Share The Ideas That Drive the World's Most Successful Companies*, (New York: Random House, 2002), x.

[25] Hiam, 31.

[26] Beth Axelrod, Helen Handfield-Jones, and Ed Michaels "A New Game Plan for C Players," *Harvard Business Review*, January 2002, 88.

[27] Dayton Fandray, "The New Thinking in Performance Appraisals," *Workforce*, May 2001, Vol. 80, Issue 5, Costa Mesa, CA., 36.

[28] Hiam, 130.

[29] Collins and Porras, 28-29.

[30] Ibid.

[31] T J Larkin and Sandar Larkin, *Communicating Change—Winning Employee Support for New Business Goals*, (New York: McGraw-Hill, Inc, 1994), xii.

[32] Axelrod, 83.

[33] Peter M. Senge, *The Fifth Discipline*, (New York: Currency/Doubleday, 1994), 139.

[34] Caruth and Handlogten, 220.

[35] Aubrey C. Daniels, *Bringing Out the Best in People: How To Apply the Astonishing Power of Positive Reinforcement*, (New York: McGraw-Hill, Inc., 2000), 5.

[36] Adapted from article written by Deborah Lambert, Utah Chapter of the National Society for Performance and Instruction, 1.21 and 1.22, referencing the work of Malcolm Knowles, *The Adult Learner: A Neglected Species*, 3rd ed. (Houston, TX: Gulf Publishing Company Book Division, 1973), quoted in "30 Things We Know For Sure About Adult Learning" by Ron and Susan Zemke, *Training/HRD Magazine*, June 1981, and the work of John M. Carroll.

[37] Beth Ann Holden, "Rating Performance," *Incentive*, New York, New York, Vol. 174, Issue 2, February 2000, 61.

[38] Robert H. Woods, *Managing Hospitality Human Resources*, 3rd ed., (Lansing, MI: Educational Institute of the American Hotel and Lodging Association, 2002), 232.

[39] Hiam, 178.

[40] Fournies, 101.

[41] Ibid., 102.

[42] Kiger, 48.

[43] Brickley et al, 46.

[44] Drucker, 370.

[45] Ibid., 372.

[46] Collins and Porras, 35.

[47] Ibid.

[48] Ibid., 37-38.

[49] Ibid., 39.

[50] Ivancevich, 102, citing Spencer Hayden, "Our Foreign Legions Are Faltering," *Personnel*, Vol. 67, Issue 8, August 1990, 40-44.

[51] Data based on the current population survey from The Bureau of Labor Statistics of the U. S. Department of Labor, press release, April 18, 2002.

[52] Fay Hansen, "Introduction: Experts Debate the Future of the FLSA and the NLRA," *Compensation & Benefits Review*, 28, July/August 1996, 6, as cited in Mondy et al, 375.

[53] David A. DeCenzo, Stephen P. Robbins, *Human Resource Management*, 6th ed., (Hoboken, NJ: Wiley and Sons, Inc., 1999), 115.

[54] Shelly Reese, "Working Around the Clock," *Business & Health* 18, April 2000, 71, as cited in Mondy et al., 374.

[55] Brian Gill, "Flextime Benefits Employees and Employers," *American Printer*, 220, February 1998, 70 as cited in Mondy et al., 375.

[56] ITAC Website and Christina Heilig, "Workshop 10—Monitoring the Program, Planning the Expansion," ITAC, 1999.

[57] Gus Manochehri and Theresa Pinkerton, "Managing Telecommuters: Opportunities and Challenges," *American Business Review*, West Haven, CT, January 2003, Vol. 21, iss. 1, 9-16.

[58] Emma Keelan, "Two for One," *Accountancy*, May 2001, London, England, 40.

[59] N. Cornelius, *Human Resource Management: A Managerial Perspective*, 2nd ed., (United Kingdom: Thompson Learning, 1999), citing Carol Norman and Robert Zwacki, "Team Appraisals-Team Approach," *Personnel Journal*, Vol. 70, Issue 9, September 1991, 101.

[60] Brickley, 148.

[61] Ibid., 148-149.

[62] Carla Joinson, "Managing Virtual Teams", *HRMagazine*, June 2002, Vol. 47, No. 6, 68.

[63] Brickley, 113.

[64] David Antonioni, "The Effects of Feedback Accountability on Upward Appraisal Ratings", *Personnel Psychology*, Summer, 1994, Vol. 47, No. 2, 349.

[65] J. H. Bernardin and R. W. Beatty, "Can Subordinates Appraisals Enhance Managerial Productivity?," *Sloan Management Review*, Vol. 28, Issue 4, Summer 1987, 70 and 71.

[66] Mark J. Vruno, "Do You Measure Up," insight-mag.com, Illinois CPA Society, October/November 2001.

[67] Bruce Pfau and Ira Kay, "Does 360-Degree Feedback Negatively Affect Company Performance?," *HRMagazine*, June 2002, Vol. 47, 58-59.

[68] Judith N. Mottl, "Appraisal Software End HR Paper Chase," *Information Week*, Manhasset, NY, November 6, 2000, 218.

[69] "The Impact of Ratee's Disability on Performance Judgments and Choice as Partner: The Role of Disability—Job Fit Stereotypes and Interdependence of Rewards." *Journal of Applied Psychology*, 1998, Vol. 83, No. 1, 102-111.

[70] Ivancevich, 384, adapted from Ron Zemke, Claire Raines and Bob Filipczak, "Generation Gaps in the Classroom," *Training*, Vol. 36, Issue 11, November 1999, 48-54.

[71] Ibid.

[72] Table 5, Bureau of Labor Statistics, U.S. Department of Labor, Civilian Labor Force by Sex, Age, Race & Hispanic origin 1990, 2000 and projected 2010 Civilian Population Survey.

[73] Louisa Wah, "Managing Gen Xers Strategically," *Management Review*, Vol. 89, Issue 3, New York, March 2000, p. 6.

[74] Ibid.

[75] Sujansky, 15.

[76] Ibid.

[77] Shannon L. Hatfield, "Understanding the Four Generations to Enhance Workplace Management," *AFP Exchange*, Vol. 22, Issue 4, Bethesda, MD, July/August 2002, 72.

Chapter 11

[1] Peter R. Scholtes, *The Leader's Handbook*, (New York: McGraw-Hill, 1998), 324.

[2] Mathis and Jackson, 381-382.

[3] Ibid, 359.

[4] Tom Coens and Mary Jenkins, *Abolishing Performance Appraisals: Why They Backfire and What To Do Instead*, (San Francisco, CA: Berrett-Koehler Publishers, Inc. 2000), 86.

[5] Scholtes, 317.

[6] Coens, 75-76.

[7] Kenneth Berrien, *General and Social Systems,* (New Jersey: Rutgers University Press, 1968), Chapter VII.

[8] Fred Nickols, "Don't Redesign Your Company's Performance Appraisal System, Scrap It!," *Corporate University Review* [home page online]; available from *http://www.traininguniversity.com*; Internet; accessed April 2000.

[9] Ibid.

[10] Coens, 40.

[11] Alfie Kohn, *Punished by Rewards: The Trouble with Gold Stars, Incentive Plans, A's, Praise, and Other Bribes,* (Boston, MA: Houghton Mifflin Company, 1993), 267.

[12] Coens, 249.

[13] Ibid., 167-169.

[14] Scholtes, 308.

[15] W. Edwards Deming, *Out of the Crisis,* (Cambridge, MA: The MIT Press, 1982), 117-118.

[16] Douglas McGregor, *The Human Side of Enterprise,* (New York: McGraw-Hill, 1960), 87.

[17] Coens, 137-138.

[18] Scholtes, 308-309.

[19] Ibid., 323.

[20] Coens, 148-149.

[21] Ibid., 30.

[22] Ibid., 170-171.

[23] Ibid., 176.

[24] Scholtes, 330.

[25] Ibid., 330.

[26] Kohn, 124-125.

[27] Ibid., 265.

[28] Scholtes, 302-303.

[29] Coens, 109-112

[30] Fandray, 40.

[31] Scholtes, 307.

[32] Coens, 249.

[33] Ibid., 249

Bibliography

Aguilar, Omar. "How Strategic Performance Management is Helping Companies Create Business Value." *Strategic Finance*, January 2003, 48.

Altmansberger, H. H., and M. Wallace. "Designing a GoalSharing Program." *American Compensation Association (ACA) Building Blocks*. Scottsdale, AZ, 1998.

Antonioni, David. "The Effects of Feedback Accountability on Upward Appraisal Ratings." *Personnel Psychology* 47 (Summer 1994): 349.

Augustine, Norman R. *Reshaping an Industry*. Massachusetts: Harvard Business School Press, 1998.

Axelrod, Beth et al. "A New Game Plan for C Players." *Harvard Business Review*, January 2002, 88.

Badaracco, Joseph C., Jr. *Leading Quietly*. Boston, MA: Harvard Business School Press, 2002.

Berger, Lance A., and Dorothy R. Berger, eds. *The Compensation Handbook*, 4th ed. New York: McGraw-Hill, 1999.

Bernardin, H. John and R. W. Beatty. "Can Subordinates Appraisals Enhance Managerial Productivity?" *Sloan Management Review* (Summer 1987): 70-71.

Bernardin, H. John, and Richard W. Beatty. *Performance Appraisal: Assessing Human Behavior at Work.* Boston, MA: Kent Publishing, 1984.

Berrien, Kenneth, *General and Social Systems.* New Jersey: Rutgers University Press, 1968.

Bois, J. Samuel. *The Art of Awareness*, 3rd ed. Iowa: Wm. C. Brown Publishers, 1979.

Brandenburger, Adam M., and Barry J. Nalebuff. *Co-opetition.* New York: Doubleday, 1996.

Brewer, Stephen J. "Aligning Human Capital in Achieving Business Goals and Strategic Objectives." SHRM White Paper, September, 2000, Reviewed March 2002.

Brickley, James A. et al. *Designing Organizations to Create Value.* New York: McGraw-Hill Companies, 2003.

Brown, H. Jackson, Jr., ed. *A Father's Book of Wisdom.* Tennessee: Rutledge Hill Press, 1988.

Buckingham, Marcus, and Curt Coffman. *First, Break All The Rules - What the World's Greatest Managers Do Differently.* New York: Simon and Schuster, 1999.

The Bureau of Labor Statistics, U. S. Department of Labor. Press Release, 18 April 2002.

Butcher, David. "It Takes Two to Review." *Management Today*, November 2002, 54-59.

Caruth, Donald L., and Gail D. Handlogten. *Managing Compensation (and Understanding It Too).* Connecticut: Quorum Books, 2001.

Cascio, Wayne F. *Managing Human Resources*, 6th ed. New York: McGraw-Hill Higher Education, 2003.

Coens, Tom, and Mary Jenkins. *Abolishing Performance Appraisals: Why They Backfire and What To Do Instead.* San Francisco, CA: Berrett-Koehler Publishers, Inc. 2000.

Collingwood, Harris and Julia Kirby. *All in a Day's Work.* Boston, MA: Harvard Business Review on Breakthrough Leadership, Harvard Business School Press, 2001.

Collins, Jim, *Good To Great.* New York: Harper Business, 2001.

Collins, James C., and Jerry I. Porras. *Building Your Company's Vision.* Boston, MA: Harvard Business Review on Change, Harvard Business School Press, 1998.

Cornelius, N. *Human Resource Management: A Managerial Perspective*, 2nd ed. United Kingdom: Thompson Learning, 1999.

Daley, Dennis M. *Strategic Human Resource Management—People and Performance Management in the Public Sector*. Upper Saddle River, NJ: Prentice Hall, 2002.

The Dallas Morning News, 22 January 2003.

Daniels, Aubrey C. *Bringing Out the Best in People: How To Apply the Astonishing Power of Positive Reinforcement*. New York: McGraw-Hill, Inc., 2000.

Davis, Brian L., et al. *The Successful Manager's Handbook— Development Suggestions for Today's Managers*. Minneapolis, MN: Personnel Decisions International, 1992.

Day, David et al. *HR Briefing*. Aspen Publishers, 1 July 2002: 7.

DeCenzo, David A., Stephen P. Robbins. *Human Resource Management*, 6th ed. Hoboken, NJ: Wiley and Sons, Inc., 1999.

Deming, W. Edwards. *Out of the Crisis*. Cambridge, MA: The MIT Press, 1982.

DeNisi, Angelo S., and Ricky W. Griffin. *Human Resource* Management. Massachusetts: Houghton Mifflin Company, 2001.

Derven, Marjorie G. "The Paradox of Performance Appraisals." *Personnel Journal* 69: 107-111.

Dolan. Shimon L. and Denis Moran. "The Effects of Rater-Ratee Relationship on Ratee Perceptions of the Appraisal Process." *Human Resource Management*, 8th ed. New York: McGraw-Hill/Irwin, 2001.

Dreher, George R and Thomas W. Dougherty. *Human Resource Strategy—A Behavioral Perspective for the General Manager*. New York: McGraw-Hill/Irwin, 2002.

Dryer, D., et al. "General Motors and Whirlpool: Two Approaches for Developing Performance Benchmarks." *HR Focus*, June 2000, 7-8.

Drucker, Peter F. *The Practice of Management*. New York: Harper Business, 1986.

Eden, Dov. *Pygmalion in Management.* Lexington, MA: Lexington Press, 1990.

Editors of The Wall Street Journal. *Boss Talk—Top CEOs Share The Ideas That Drive the World's Most Successful Companies.* New York: Random House, 2002.

Fandray, Dayton. "The New Thinking in Performance Appraisals." *Workforce* 80 (May 2001): 36.

Farkas, Charles M. and Suzy Wetlaufer. *The Way Chief Executive Officers Lead*. Boston, MA: Harvard Business Review on Leadership, Harvard Business School Press, 1998.

Fisher, Liz. "Thou Shalt Not Fail, Balanced Scorecard Implementation, 10 Commandments from KPMG." *Accountancy International,* September 1998, cited in "Balanced Scorecard Basics on Implementation," by Valerie E. Pike, December 2000, Reviewed March 2002, SHRM White Paper.

Fournies, Ferdinand F. *Coaching*. New York: McGraw-Hill, 2000.

Gerstle, C. Andrew. "Heroic Honor: Chikamatsu and the Samurai Ideal." *Harvard Journal of Asiatic Studies*, December 1997, 307.

Gerstner, Louis V. *Who Says Elephants Can't Dance*. New York: Harper Business, 2002.

Gill, Brian. "Flextime Benefits Employees and Employers." *American Printer* 220 (February 1998): 70.

Gittell, Jody Hoffer. *The Southwest Airlines Way*. New York: McGraw-Hill, 2003.

Hall, Edward T. *The Silent Language*. New York: Anchor Books, 1990.

Halpert, Jane et al. "Pregnancy as a Source of Bias in Performance Appraisals." *Journal of Organizational Behavior* 14 (1993): 655.

Hansen, Fay. "Introduction: Experts Debate the Future of the FLSA and the NLRA." *Compensation & Benefits Review* 28, (July/August 1996), 6.

Harari, Oren. *The Leadership Secrets of Colin Powell*. New York: McGraw-Hill, 2002.

Hatfield, Shannon L. "Understanding the Four Generations to Enhance Workplace Management." *AFP Exchange* 22, (July/August 2002): 72.

Hayes, Mary. "Goal Oriented." *Information Week*, 10 March 2003, 35.

Hays, Scott. "Pros and Cons of Pay for Performance," *ZPG* [home page online]; available from *http://www.zigonperf.com/resources/pmnews/proscons.html*; Internet; accessed 14 April 2003.

Heathfield, Susan. "Performance Appraisals Don't Work." *Human Resources* [home page online]; available from *http://www.humanresources.guide@about.com*, Internet; accessed June 2000.

Hedge, Jerry W. and Michael J. Kavanagh. "Improving the Accuracy of Performance Evaluations: Comparisons of Three Methods of Performance Appraiser Training." *Journal of Applied Psychology*, 68-73, in *Human Resource Management* (8th ed.), John M. Ivancevich, McGraw-Hill/Irwin, NY, 2001, 268.

Hiam, Alex. *Making Horses Drink*. Irvine, CA: Entrepreneur Media, Inc., 2002.

Holden, Beth Ann. "Rating Performance." *Incentive* 174 (February 2000): 61.

Hopkins, Bill L., and Thomas C. Mawhinney, eds. *Pay for Performance*. New York: The Haworth Press, Inc., 1992.

"The Impact of Ratee's Disability on Performance Judgments and Choice as Partner: The Role of Disability—Job Fit Stereotypes and Interdependence of Rewards." *Journal of Applied Psychology* 83 (1998): 102-111.

ITAC Website and Christina Heilig. "Workshop 10—Monitoring the Program, Planning the Expansion." ITAC, 1999.

Ivancevich, John M., citing Spencer Hayden. "Our Foreign Legions Are Faltering." *Personnel*, August 1990, 40-44.

————. citing Mary N. Vinson. "The Pros and Cons of 360-Degree Feedback: Making It Work." *Training and Development*, April 1996, 11-12.

Jacoby, Sanford M. "A Century of Human Resource Management." Paper presented at 75th Anniversary Conference of Industrial Relations Counselors, Princeton University, 11 September 2001.

Jacoby, Sanford. *Employing Bureaucracy: Masters to Managers: Historical and Comparative Perspectives on American Employers*. New York: Columbia University Press, 1991.

Jacoby, Sanford ed. *Masters to Managers*. New York: Columbia University Press, 1991.

Jerome, Paul J. *Coaching Through Effective Feedback - A Practical Guide to Successful Communication*. California: Richard Chang Associates, Jossey-Bass/Pfeiffer, 1994.

Joinson, Carla. "Managing Virtual Teams." *HRMagazine* 47 (June 2002).

Kaplan, Robert S., and David P. Norton. *The Balanced Scorecard*. Boston, MA: Harvard Business School Press, 1996.

Keelan, Emma. "Two for One." *Accountancy* (May 2001): 40.

"Keep Your Staff—Even Without the Big Pay Increases." *Accounting Office Management & amp; Administration Report*, available from *http://www.smartbiz.com/article/view/176* [home page online]; Internet; accessed May 2003.

Kiger, Patrick J. "Optimas 2001 - Vision: Frequent Employee Feedback Is Worth The Cost And Time." *Workforce* 80, March 2001, 62.

Knowles, Malcolm. *The Adult Learner: A Neglected Species*, 3rd ed. Houston, TX: Gulf Publishing Company Book Division, 1973.

Kohn, Alfie. *Punished by Rewards: The Trouble with Gold Stars, Incentive Plans, A's, Praise, and Other Bribes*. Boston, MA: Houghton Mifflin Company, 1993.

Kotter, John P. "Winning at Change." *Leader to Leader* 10 (Fall 1998): 27-33.

Kovach, Kenneth A. *Strategic Human Resources Management*. Maryland: University Press of America, 1996.

Lambert, Deborah. Utah Chapter of the National Society for Performance and Instruction, 1.21 and 1.22.

Larkin, T J, and Sandar Larkin. *Communicating Change—Winning Employee Support for New Business Goals*. New York: McGraw-Hill, Inc, 1994.

Lawrie, J. "Prepare For a Performance Appraisal." *Personnel Journal* 69: 132-136.

LeDoux, Joseph. *The Emotional Brain*. New York: Touchstone/Simon & Schuster, 1986.

Lukas, Paul. "The Great American Company." *Fortune Small Business*, 19 March 2003.

Manochehri, Gus and Theresa Pinkerton. "Managing Telecommuters: Opportunities and Challenges." *American Business Review* 21 (January 2003): 9-16.

Mathis, Robert L., and John H Jackson. *Human Resources Management*, 10th ed. Mason, OH: South-Western College Publications, 2003.

Maxwell, John C. *The 17 Essential Qualities of A Team Player*. Tennessee: Thomas Nelson Publishers, 2002.

McGregor, Douglas. *The Human Side of Enterprise*. New York: McGraw-Hill, 1960.

McKay, Matthew et al. *Messages*, California: New Harbinger Publications, Inc., 1995.

McKirchey, Karen, *Powerful Performance Appraisals*. New Jersey: Career Press, 1998.

Milkovich, George T. and Jerry M. Newman. *Compensation*, 6th ed. Boston, MA: McGraw-Hill/Irwin, 1999.

Mintzberg, Henry. *The Manager's Job*. Massachusetts: Harvard Business School Press, 1998.

Moehrie, Thomas G. "The Evolution of Compensation in a Changing Economy." *Issue of Compensation and Working Conditions* 6 (Fall 2001): 10.

Moglia, Tony. *Partners in Performance, Successful Performance Management*. California: Crisp Publications, Inc., 1997.

Mondy, Wayne R., et al. *Human Resource Management*, 8th ed., New Jersey: Prentice Hall, 2002.

Mottl, Judith N. "Appraisal Software End HR Paper Chase." *Information Week*, 6 November 2000, 218.

Nelson, Bob. *1001 Ways to Reward Employees*. New York: Workman Publishing, 1994.

Newman, Edwin. *Strictly Speaking*. New York: The Bobbs-Merrill Company, 1974.

Nickols, Fred. "Don't Redesign Your Company's Performance Appraisal System, Scrap It!" *Corporate University Review* [home page online]; available from *http://www.traininguniversity.com*; Internet; accessed April 2000.

Noe, Raymond, et al. *Human Resource Management - Gaining a Competitive Advantage*, 3rd ed. New York: McGraw-Hill/Irwin, 2000.

Parks, Susan. "Improving Workplace Performance: Historical and Theoretical Contexts." *Monthly Labor Review*, May 1995, 20.

Pfau, Bruce and Ira Kay. "Does 360-Degree Feedback Negatively Affect Company Performance?" *HRMagazine* 47 (June 2002): 58-59.

Pfeffer, Jeffrey. *Six Dangerous Myths About Pay*. Boston, MA: Harvard Business Review on Managing People, Harvard Business School Press, 1999.

Pfeffer, Jeffrey, and C. O'Reilly III. *Hidden Value: How Great Companies Achieve Extraordinary Results with Ordinary People*. Boston, MA: Harvard Business School Press, 2000.

Pulakos, E.D. "The Development of Training Programs to Increase Accuracy on Different Rating Forms." *Organizational Behavior and Human Decision Processes* 38 (1986): 76-91.

Redman, T., et al. "Performance Appraisal in an NHS Hospital." *Human Resource Management Journal* 10 (2002): 48-62.

Reese, Shelly. "Working Around the Clock." *Business & Health* 18 (April 2000); 71.

Satterfield, Terry. "Speaking of Pay." *HR Magazine* 48, (March 2003): 99-101.

Schaffer, Robert H. and Harvey A. Thomson. "Successful Change Programs Begin with Results." *Harvard Business Review on Change* 70 (January 1992): 80.

Scholtes, Peter R. *The Leader's Handbook*. New York: McGraw-Hill, 1998.

———. "Total Quality or Performance Appraisal: Choose One." *National Productivity Review* 12 (Summer 1993): 349.

Schrage, Michael. "Shared Minds: The New Technologies of Collaboration." interview in *The Washington Post* by Don Oldenburg, 12 March 1991, E5.

Schroder, Ingo W. "The Political Economy of Common Destinies in the American Indian Southwest." *Journal of the Southwest*, Spring 2002, 3.

Schwenk, Albert E. and Jordan N. Pfuntner. "Compensation in the Later Part of the Century. "*Issue of Compensation and Working Conditions* 6 (Fall 2001): 1.

Segal, Jonathan A. "Fine-Tune Performance Appraisals to Make Them Effective—and Less Arduous." SHRM Managing Smart, 1 Quarter 2001.

Senge, Peter M. *The Fifth Discipline*. New York: Currency/Doubleday, 1994.

Shinkman, Christopher J. "Performance Appraisal: A Positive Approach." *AFP Exchange* 21 (March/April 2001): 78-80.

Smither, James W., ed. *Performance Appraisal: State of the Art in Practice*. San Francisco, CA: John Wiley & Sons, Inc., 1998.

Span, Paula. "Marriage At First Sight." *Washington Post Magazine*, 23 February 2003, 20.

Sujansky, Joanne. "The Critical Care and Feeding of Generation Y," *Workforce*, May 2002, 15.

Swan, William S. *How To Do a Superior Performance Appraisal*. New York: John Wiley & Sons, 1991.

Table 5, Bureau of Labor Statistics, U.S. Department of Labor, *Civilian Labor Force by Sex, Age, Race & Hispanic Origin 1990, 2000 and projected 2010 Civilian Population Survey*.

Tannen, Dr. Deborah. *That's Not What I Meant*. New York: Ballantine Books, 1986.

Tesdell, Dennis R. "The Top Ten Fears That Keep People From Getting What They Want In Life." Adapted from *CoachVille Resource Center*, *http://www.coachville.com*, 1998.

Toffler, Alvin. *Powershift*. New York: Bantam Books, Bantam Doubleday Dell Publishing Group, 1990.

Vruno, Mark J. "Do You Measure Up." *insight-mag.com* (October/November 2001).

Wah, Louisa. "Managing Gen Xers Strategically." *Management Review* 89 (March 2000): 6.

Woods, Robert H. *Managing Hospitality Human Resources*, 3rd ed. Lansing, MI: Educational Institute of the American Hotel and Lodging Association, 2002.

Zemke, Ron, et al. "Generation Gaps in the Classroom." *Training* (November 1999), 48-54.

Zemke, Ron and Susan Zemke. "30 Things We Know For Sure About Adult Learning." *Training/HRD Magazine* (June 1981).

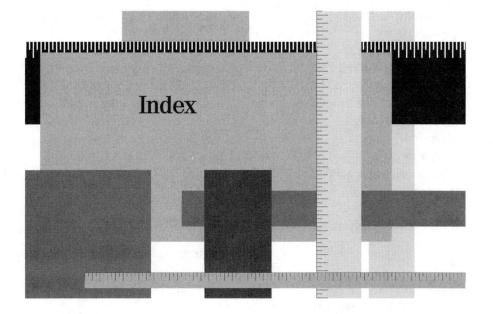

Index

About the Authors

SHARON ARMSTRONG began her career in Human Resources in 1985 as a recruiter/trainer in a large Manhattan law firm. Since then, she has served as a Director of Human Resources at another law firm and three nonprofit associations in Washington, D.C. Her responsibilities always included oversight of the performance management system.

Since launching her own consulting business, Human Resources 911, in 1998, Armstrong has consulted with many large corporations and small businesses. She has provided training and completed HR projects dealing with performance management design and implementation for a wide variety of clients in the profit and nonprofit sectors, as well as government settings. She received her bachelor's degree from the University of Southern Maine and her master's degree in Counseling from George Washington University. She is a certified Professional in Human Resources.

Sharon is the coauthor of a humor book, *Heeling the Canine Within: The Dog's Self-Help Companion*.

MADELYN APPELBAUM is a strategic communications professional who has managed wide-ranging initiatives on national and international levels. She has been published in many U.S. newspapers and, early in her career, honed her skills as an investigative journalist. Her editorial and film products have been national award winners. Overseeing performance appraisals for several departments, she developed an interactive tool designed to make performance appraisals a two-way process by factoring employee feedback in upfront. Madelyn's communication expertise spans 30 years, during which she has also effectively marketed many of the editorial products she has developed.

Appelbaum has served on the faculty of George Washington University in Washington, DC. She attended St. Joseph's University and The Annenberg Graduate School for Communication, University of Pennsylvania. She is coauthor of the book, *Enjoy Philadelphia*.